辱虐管理与员工主动行为研究

许 勤 著

A STUDY OF
ABUSIVE SUPERVISION AND
EMPLOYEE
PROACTIVE BEHAVIOR

图书在版编目（CIP）数据

辱虐管理与员工主动行为研究／许勤著．—北京：经济管理出版社，2020.11
ISBN 978-7-5096-7643-1

Ⅰ.①辱⋯　Ⅱ.①许⋯　Ⅲ.①人事管理—研究　Ⅳ.①D035.2

中国版本图书馆 CIP 数据核字（2020）第 235232 号

组稿编辑：赵亚荣
责任编辑：赵亚荣
责任印制：黄章平
责任校对：陈　颖

出版发行：经济管理出版社
　　　　　（北京市海淀区北蜂窝 8 号中雅大厦 A 座 11 层　100038）
网　　址：www.E-mp.com.cn
电　　话：(10) 51915602
印　　刷：唐山玺诚印务有限公司
经　　销：新华书店
开　　本：720mm×1000mm /16
印　　张：9.25
字　　数：202 千字
版　　次：2021 年 5 月第 1 版　2021 年 5 月第 1 次印刷
书　　号：ISBN 978-7-5096-7643-1
定　　价：58.00 元

·版权所有　翻印必究·
凡购本社图书，如有印装错误，由本社读者服务部负责调换。
联系地址：北京阜外月坛北小街 2 号
电话：(10) 68022974　　邮编：100836

前　言

员工主动行为（Proactive Behavior）是一种面向未来的、主动自发的、预见性的工作行为。对于现代组织来说，这种工作行为非常重要，因为它们处在变化迅速、竞争激烈和高度不确定的环境中。因此，在过去的二十年中，探索员工主动行为预测因素的研究快速增加。一些学者发现，主管在激发员工的主动行为方面可以发挥重要的作用。在回顾现有文献后，本书发现了一些有待进一步研究之处。当前的研究主要集中在积极的主管行为的影响上，例如主管的支持和主管的变革型行为。在实际工作中，主管可能是辱虐性的或破坏性的（Einarsen, Aasland & Skogstad, 2007），但这在主动行为文献中并未得到足够的重视。此外，虽然辱虐管理研究已经假设并检验了组织认同对辱虐管理作用的调节效应，但是研究结论并不一致。

为了解决这些问题，本书以压力交互模型（Transactional Model of Stress）为理论基础，提出辱虐管理会消耗下属的资源并分散他们的工作精力，因此会降低下属的主动行为频率，以及辱虐管理与组织认同的交互作用会受到员工的积极情感特质的调节。换句话说，组织认同感较低的下属如果具有积极的情感特质，主管给予辱虐待遇时则会遭受最大的影响。本书包含两项子研究。子研究1侧重于一般主动性或个人主动性，并收集了国内两家医院的165位牙医和41位直接主管的样本。数据分析结果表明，辱虐管理与个人主动性负相关，并且当组织认同较低与正向情感特质较高时，辱虐管理与个人主动性的负相关关系最强。为了拓展并重复检验子研究1的发现，子研究2使用了另一种主动行为的测量量表，然后调查了国内一家大型交通运输公司中的226对员工与主管。结果表明，辱虐管理只与主管导向的主动行为负相关，辱虐管理、组织认同与正向情感特质的三维交互作用与三种主动行为都显著正相关。最后，本书讨论了理论和实践启示，并指出了一些未来的研究方向。

本书包括以下五章内容：第1章介绍了本书研究的创新之处、所探讨的研究问题和预期的贡献。第2章描述了主动行为的历史背景、定义、类型和目标，系统地回顾了前因、作用机制、边界条件和后果的已有成果，最后总结了主动行为研究中存在的问题。第3章是本书的核心部分，以压力的交互模型为基础，分析了辱虐管理与员工主动行为之间的关系，以及组织认同和正向情感特质如何共同调节上述关系。第4章分别介绍了两个子研究的研究方法（样本特征、数据收集过程、变量测量和分析策略）及数据分析结果。第5章概述了两个子研究的结果，讨论了本书的理论和实践意义、局限性和未来的研究方向，并为本书做了总结。

本书不仅对我国企事业单位中辱虐管理与员工主动行为的关系进行了系统性的研究，而且通过使用我国医院和交通运输公司两个样本检验了这种关系，并为这两个行业提供了有针对性的建议和启示。希望本书的出版不仅能对促进员工主动行为在我国的研究进展具有推动作用，而且能对有效提高中国企业员工的积极主动性提供切实有用的指导意见。

PREFACE

Proactive behavior refers to anticipatory, future-or change-oriented, and self-starting behaviors at work. Such behavior is very important for modern organizations because they are facing fast change, fierce competition and great uncertainty. Thus, there has been a surge of research on identifying the predictors of proactivity over the past two decades. Among these, it has been noted that supervisors can play a critical role in promoting employee proactive behavior. Several research gaps, however, are identified after reviewing the extant literature. Firstly, current research has mainly focused on the impact of positive supervisor behaviors such as supervisor support and supervisor's transformational leader behaviors. In reality, supervisors can be abusive or destructive (Einarsen, Aasland & Skogstad, 2007), and this aspect has not gained adequate attention in the proactivity literature. Additionally, although abusive supervision research has theorized and tested the moderating role of organizational identification in influencing how subordinates respond to supervisory abuse, the extant results are not consistent.

To address these gaps, the present study draws from the transactional model of stress (Lazarus & Folkman, 1984, 1987), and argues that abusive supervisors will deplete subordinates' resources and distract them from their tasks, and as a result, will lower subordinates' frequencies of proactive behaviors, and that the interactive effect of abusive supervision and organizational identification on employee proactivity will be contingent on individual affective disposition (positive trait affectivity). In other words, subordinates with low organizational identification will suffer more from abusive supervision if they are high in positive trait affectivity.

I conducted two multisource sub-studies to test the above hypotheses. In Study 1, I focused on general proactivity, that is, personal initiative. Using data from a sample of 165 dentists and their immediate supervisors from two hospitals, I found that abusive supervision was negatively associated with personal initiative, and when organizational identification was low and positive affectivity was high, the relationship between abusive supervision and personal initiative was the most negative. In Study 2, I used different measures of proactive behaviors (i.e., organizational, supervisory and coworker-directed proactive behaviors) to test the robustness and generalizability of the findings in Study 1. Data were collected from 226 employees and their direct supervisors of a large transportation company in China. The results showed that abusive supervision was only negatively associated with supervisory proactive behavior and the three-way interaction of abusive supervision, organizational identification and positive affectivity on three forms of proactive behaviors were all significant. Finally, this study summarizes the main findings, discusses the theoretical and practical implications, and indicates limitations and future research directions.

This book mainly includes five chapters outlined as follows. The first chapter introduces theoretical gaps, research questions and intended contributions of this study. The second chapter describes the historical background, definition, type and target of proactive behavior, systematically reviews the current findings on antecedents, motivational processes, boundary conditions and consequences, and finally summarizes the emerging issues in proactive behavior research. Chapter 3, the core part of this study, draws from the transactional model of stress, and analyzes how abusive supervision relates to employee proactive behavior and how organizational identification and positive affectivity jointly moderate the above relationship. Chapter 4 respectively presents research method (i.e., the sample, procedure, measures and analytic strategy) and data analysis results of two sub-studies. The final chapter provides an overview of the findings for two sub-studies, discusses the theoretical and practical implications, limitations and future research directions, and makes conclusions for the study.

This book not only conducted a systematic study on the association between abusive supervision and proactive behavior, but examined such relationship by using two different samples such as hospitals and transportation corporations, and provides suggestions and implications for these two industries. It is hoped that the publication of this book not only has theoretical significance to promote the study of employee proactive behavior in China, but also has a practical guiding role in promoting the improvement of employees' proactivity in Chinese enterprises.

目 录

1 引言

1.1 现有理论有待进一步研究之处 ………………………… 2
1.2 研究问题 …………………………………………………… 6
1.3 预期贡献 …………………………………………………… 6

2 文献综述

2.1 主动行为的历史背景 ……………………………………… 9
2.2 主动行为的概念内涵 ……………………………………… 11
2.3 主动行为的类型 …………………………………………… 13
2.4 主动行为的目标 …………………………………………… 15
2.5 主动行为的前因变量 ……………………………………… 18
    2.5.1 情境类前因变量 …………………………………… 18
    2.5.2 个体类前因变量 …………………………………… 23
2.6 中介机制 …………………………………………………… 25
    2.6.1 能力动机 …………………………………………… 26
    2.6.2 缘由动机 …………………………………………… 27
    2.6.3 情绪动机 …………………………………………… 29

2.7 边界条件 ·· 30
2.8 主动行为的结果变量 ································ 31
2.9 主动行为研究的现存问题 ·························· 33
　　2.9.1 辱虐管理的作用 ····························· 33
　　2.9.2 潜在的调节变量 ····························· 36

3 理论基础与假设提出

3.1 压力的交互模型 ······································ 38
3.2 辱虐管理与主动行为 ································ 40
3.3 组织认同与正向情感特质的作用 ················· 42
　　3.3.1 组织认同 ·· 43
　　3.3.2 正向情感特质 ································· 46
3.4 辱虐管理、组织认同与正向情感特质的三维交互作用 ········ 48

4 研究方法与设计

4.1 研究概述 ·· 51
4.2 子研究1 ·· 52
　　4.2.1 样本和流程 ····································· 52
　　4.2.2 测量 ·· 54
　　4.2.3 分析方法 ·· 55
　　4.2.4 研究结果 ·· 56
　　4.2.5 讨论 ·· 60
4.3 子研究2 ·· 61
　　4.3.1 样本和流程 ····································· 64
　　4.3.2 测量 ·· 64

4.3.3 分析方法 ……………………………………… 65
　　4.3.4 研究结果 ……………………………………… 66
　　4.3.5 讨论 …………………………………………… 74

5 研究结论与展望

5.1 结果概述 …………………………………………… 75
5.2 理论意义 …………………………………………… 77
5.3 实践意义 …………………………………………… 80
5.4 研究局限 …………………………………………… 82
5.5 未来研究方向 ……………………………………… 85
5.6 研究总结 …………………………………………… 87

参考文献 ………………………………………………… 89

附录 A …………………………………………………… 115

附录 B …………………………………………………… 124

附录 C …………………………………………………… 129

后记 ……………………………………………………… 131

TABLE OF CONTENTS

1. AN INTRODUCTION OF THE STUDY

1.1 Theoretical Gaps 2
1.2 Research Questions 6
1.3 Intended Contributions 6

2. LITERATURE REVIEW ON PROACTIVE BEHAVIOR

2.1 Historical Background 9
2.2 Definition of Proactive Behavior 11
2.3 Type of Proactive Behavior 13
2.4 Target of Proactive Behavior 15
2.5 Antecedents of Employee Proactive Behavior 18
    2.5.1 Situational Antecedents 18
    2.5.2 Individual Antecedents 23
2.6 Motivational Processes 25
    2.6.1 "Can Do" Motivational Process 26
    2.6.2 "Reason To" Motivational Process 27
    2.6.3 "Energized To" Motivational Process 29

2.7	Boundary Conditions	30
2.8	Consequences of Employee Proactive Behavior	31
2.9	Emerging Issues in Proactive Behavior Research	33
	2.9.1 Role of Abusive Supervision	33
	2.9.2 Potential Moderators	36

3 THEORETICAL BACKGROUND AND HYPOTHESES DEVELOPMENT

3.1	Transactional Model of Stress	38
3.2	Abusive Supervision and Proactive Behavior	40
3.3	The Roles of Organizational Identification and Positive Affectivity	42
	3.3.1 Organizational Identification	43
	3.3.2 Positive Affectivity	46
3.4	The Three-Way Effects of Abusive Supervision, Organizational Identification and Positive Affectivity	48

4 METHODOLOGY AND RESEARCH DESIGN

4.1	Overview of the Two Studies	51
4.2	Study 1	52
	4.2.1 Sample and Procedure	52
	4.2.2 Measures	54
	4.2.3 Analytical Approach	55
	4.2.4 Results	56
	4.2.5 Discussion	60
4.3	Study 2	61

4.3.1	Sample and Procedure	64
4.3.2	Measures	64
4.3.3	Analytical Approach	65
4.3.4	Results	66
4.3.5	Discussion	74

5 GENERAL DISCUSSION

5.1	Overview of Findings	75
5.2	Theoretical Implications	77
5.3	Practical Implications	80
5.4	Limitations	82
5.5	Future Research Directions	85
5.6	Conclusions	87

REFERENCES 89

APPENDIX A 115

APPENDIX B 124

APPENDIX C 129

POSTSCRIPT 131

AN INTRODUCTION OF THE STUDY

Employee proactivity is very important in modern organizations, where there is ambiguous environment, rapid technology changes, and fierce global competition (Crant, 2000; Grant & Ashford, 2008; Parker & Collins, 2010). Proactive employees can anticipate the future, act in advance and be innovative, thereby not only getting superior performance and high job satisfaction, but rendering organizations achieve the competitive edge (Griffin, Neal & Parker, 2007; Wanberg & Kammeyer-Mueller, 2000). Therefore, not surprisingly, academic researchers have explored widely the antecedents of proactivity at work (e. g., Chen, Farh, Campbell-Bush, Wu & Wu, 2013; Liu, Zhu & Yang, 2010; Love & Dustin, 2014; Raub & Liao, 2012; Seibert, Kraimer & Crant, 2001).

Among these, supervisors are suggested to play a critical role in predicting subordinates' proactive behaviors (e. g., Detert & Burris, 2007; Rank, Nelson, Allen & Xu, 2009). However, researchers have mainly focused on the positive side of a supervisor, such as supervisory transformational leadership (Strauss, Griffin & Rafferty, 2009), ethical behaviors (Avey, Wernsing & Palanski, 2012), and supportive supervision (Parker, Williams & Turner, 2006). In reality, supervisors do not always act in a positive and encouraging manner (De Cremer, 2003). They may abuse their subordinates, withhold needed information, and humiliate or ridicule them in front of others (Aryee, Chen, Sun & Debrah,

2007; Tepper, 2000). However, limited attention has been paid to examine the influence of such kind of supervisory abuse on subordinate proactive behavior. According to Tornau and Frese (2012), "the field requires additional research relating proactivity concepts to leadership" (p. 35). Therefore, this study investigates how abusive supervision is related to subordinate proactive behavior.

More importantly, proactivity literature has emphasized that the effect of situational antecedents on proactivity may be contingent and called for research to "further identify under which circumstances situational influences may promote or inhibit proactive behaviors at work" (Bindl & Parker, 2011, p. 50). Echoed from abusive supervision literature, it is important and necessary to explore the boundary conditions under which abusive supervision has a stronger or weaker influence on subordinate work outcomes (for reviews, see Martinko, Harvey, Brees & Mackey, 2013; Tepper, 2007). Therefore, I further examine possible boundary conditions for the relationship between abusive supervision and subordinate proactive behavior.

In sum, it is useful to explore how and when abusive supervision may influence employee proactive behavior. This study attempts to advance our understanding of these critical issues.

1.1 Theoretical Gaps

Given the importance of proactive behavior, substantial efforts have been put into exploring its predictors, mechanisms and boundary conditions. Turning to the supervisory leadership aspect, researchers have mainly examined the impact of positive forms of supervisory behaviors, such as supervisors' transformational leadership, leader-member exchange, and supervisory support (e.g., Belschak & Den Hartog, 2010; Yang & Liu, 2014; Yuan & Woodman, 2010).

However, more is unknown about the role of supervisors in influencing subordinates' proactive actions. This study aims to fill a few theoretical gaps as follows.

First, it is suggested that the effect of abusive supervision on subordinate proactive behavior has been under-examined (Burris, Detert & Chiaburu, 2008). As mentioned above, abusive supervision includes behaviors that criticize publicly, humiliate subordinates; it is also destructive. Although it is a low base-rate phenomenon, it has been found to have tremendous impacts on employee work outcomes (Martinko et al., 2013), as well as group performance and behaviors (Priesemuth, Schminke, Ambrose & Folger, 2014). It is possible that, supervisory abuse depletes subordinates' physical and cognitive resources, thus leading to fewer proactive behaviors.

Thus far, there has been a paucity of similar empirical studies (e.g., Burris et al., 2008; Li, Ling & Liu, 2009; Rafferty & Restubog, 2011). Nonetheless, most of them have focused on voice as the dependent variable. Because researchers have suggested that voice can be reactive (Van Dyne & Le Pine, 1998), the findings of these studies cannot be easily generalized to other types of proactive behaviors. Moreover, Burris et al. (2008) called for more research on voice toward other targets such as coworkers. Therefore, there is a lack of empirical investigation on the relationships between abusive supervision and general proactivity as well as proactive behavior directed at different targets.

Second, in proactivity literature, not much attention has been devoted to explore under what circumstances situational antecedents are more strongly or negatively associated with consequences. For example, Bindl and Parker (2011) have stressed the necessity of exploring boundary conditions for situational influences on self-initiated behaviors. More relevantly, Grant and Ashford (2008) have theorized that the relationship between ambiguity, a workplace stressor, and proactivity is contingent on individual differences. Indeed, empirical studies of Fuller et al. (2006) and Grant and Rothbard (2013) revealed a nonsignificant relationship between ambiguity and proactivity. Thus, it is of significance to follow this lead and empirically test the moderators of the influence of workplace stressors. Of those relevant studies, only one study has taken the first step to examine the moderating role of perceived supervisory status in the abusive supervision-voice link. Hence, it is necessary to further identify the possible moderators of the abusive supervision and proactive behavior association.

Organizational identification, the extent to which employees feel belongingness to an organization and incorporate attributes of the organization in their self-concept (Ashforth & Mael, 1989; Dutton, Dukerich & Harquail, 1994), has been argued to be a "root construct" in organizational studies. It has been demonstrated that employees who highly identify with their organization are more concentrated on their work, thereby performing more self-initiated actions. Furthermore, employees with high organizational identification tend to receive more support from colleagues, and thus, may have more resources left to perform anticipatory and change-oriented behaviors. Hereto, it is reasonable to explore the moderating role of organizational identification that accounts for the relationship between abusive supervision and proactive behavior.

Drawing from the stress literature, to date, only a few studies have focused on the moderating role of organizational identification on the stressor – consequences links (Decoster, Camps, Stouten, Vandevyvere & Tripp, 2013; Harris, Kacmar & Zivnuska, 2007; Reilly, 1994; Xu, Xi, Zhao & Li, 2015), but their results were inconsistent. For example, Decoster et al. (2013) argued that the more an individual identified with the organization, the more meaningful he or she would perceive work was. Thus, in the situation of an abusive supervisor, identified employees would react in a more positive way. Using a sample of 134 employee-supervisor dyads, they found support for this buffering hypothesis. On the contrary, Xu et al. (2015) obtained data from 456 employees and 78 human resource managers, and found that abused by supervisors, employees who highly identified with and committed to their organization were more likely to act negatively by withholding their concerns and suggestions. Likewise, Harris and colleagues (2007) theorized that employees who valued their work in the organization might spend extra effort coping with their abusive supervisor, and consequently, reacted more negatively. Using a sample of 209 employees from an automotive company, they found support for this prediction. Therefore, it is possible that the moderating role of organizational identification in the abusive supervision-outcomes associations is also contingent.

Underpinned by transaction model of stress (Lazarus & Folkman, 1984, 1987), how an individual responds to stressful situations should rely not only on his or her beliefs and goals, but also on his or her dispositions. Trait positive affectivity refers to an individual's general tendency to experience, either in terms of intensity or frequency, positive emotions across situations (Watson & Clark, 1992). A few studies to date have suggested that individuals with high positive affectivity are enthusiastic, and socially potent, thereby engaging in more proactive behaviors (Bindl & Parker, 2012; Den Hartog & Belschak, 2007). In addition, extant organizational research has investigated the impact of positive affectivity on stress-related processes (i.e., Duffy, Ganster & Shaw, 1998; Harvey, Stoner, Hochwarter & Kacmar, 2007; Hochwarter, Kiewitz, Castro, Perrewé & Ferris, 2003). However, to my knowledge, no research has investigated whether subordinate positive affectivity moderates the effect of organizational identification on the abusive supervision-proactive behavior link.

To conclude, by utilizing voice as a specific type of proactive behavior, some researchers have examined the effect of abusive supervision on voice to supervisors. The impact of abusive supervision on general proactive behavior as well as proactive behaviors directed at several targets needs further theoretical and empirical investigation. The roles of subordinate organizational identification and positive affectivity are extremely important for such impact. In order to extend previous work on proactive behavior and abusive supervision, a fine-grained interactional model is proposed to be developed here to simultaneously include these factors.

1.2 Research Questions

As discussed above, this study aims tosolve the following research questions: (1) how is abusive supervision, as a workplace stressor, related to subordinate proactive behavior? (2) When is abusive supervision particularly ineffective in predicting proactive behavior? This study takes a stress perspective (Lazarus & Folkman, 1984, 1987), and proposes a fine-grained interactive model to address these gaps and questions. In this model, abusive supervision is negatively related to subordinate proactive behavior. Moreover, abusive supervision interacts with organizational identification and positive affectivity to predict proactive behavior.

Two sub-studies were conducted to test my hypotheses. In study 1, I collected data from a sample of dentists for the predictors (i.e., abusive supervision, organizational identification, and positive affectivity) as well as their immediate supervisors for the outcome variable (i.e., personal initiative). In Study 2, I used a sample of employees from a large transportation company for the same predictors and their direct supervisors for the outcome variables (i.e., organizational proactive behavior, supervisory proactive behavior and coworker-directed proactive behavior), to make this research more robust and generalizable.

1.3 Intended Contributions

By focusing on the roles of abusive supervision, organizational identification and positive affectivity and the effect of the three-way interaction on proactive behavior, this study attempts to make three major contributions to the literature. First, I answer the critical research question: how is abusive supervision related to proactive behavior? Albeit it has been found that abusive supervision is negatively associated with voice towards supervisors and organizations, I seek to advance our understanding of the effect of abusive supervision on proactivity by focusing on personal initiative and proactive behaviors directed at organization, supervisor and coworkers as the dependent variables. This study also extends previous research (such as Belschak & Den Hartog, 2011; Griffin et al., 2007) by theorizing supervisor is an unnegligible target of proactive behavior and examining proactivity directed at the organization, supervisor and coworkers simultaneously. Moreover, my investigation of various proactivity concepts as dependent variables attempts to answer Tornau and Frese's (2012) call for "include more than one proactivity concept" in their studies (p. 35).

Second, I aim to extend the literature by exploring the moderating role of subordinate characteristics in the abusive supervision-proactive behavior associations. In this study, organizational identification is first argued to be one moderator. This is in line with prior research on the moderating effect of organizational identification on the relationship between abusive supervision and cohesion and gossip (e.g., Decoster et al., 2013). However, based on the evidence from stress literature, the moderating effect of organizational identification may be dependent on subordinate positive affectivity. By doing so, I deepen our understanding of the abusive supervision-proactivity relationship and address the call for exploring boundary conditions of the role of situational antecedents in proactivity studies.

Finally, this study makes a contribution to the literature on proactive behavior and abusive supervision by building a more fine-grained interactional model. By hypothesizing and testing an interaction of abusive supervision, organizational identification and positive affectivity in relation to subordinate proactivity, I extend previous research on abusive supervision and proactive behavior (e. g., Burris et al., 2008; Decoster et al., 2013; Li et al., 2009). I suggest that how an employee views their membership in an organization may impact the effect of the situational factor (e. g., abusive supervision) on the employee's proactivity, depending on individual difference such as positive affectivity.

LITERATURE REVIEW ON PROACTIVE BEHAVIOR

This chapter provides a historical review of traditional work motivation theories and focuses on employee proactivity. Then, I clarify the conceptualization of proactive behavior in terms of definition, target and type, and present an overview of the nomological network of employee proactive behavior. Finally, I advance the literature by suggesting that abusive supervision plays a critical role in influencing employee proactivity, and that this association has boundary conditions, that is, it is dependent on the joint effects of organizational identification and positive affectivity.

2.1 Historical Background

Proactive behavior, as a particular type of motivated behavior, slowly stems from traditional work motivation theories (Bateman & Crant, 1993). The early motivational theories were conceptualized on the basis of the orthodox principles of behaviorism. Employees were viewed as passive recipients of workplace arrangements, which were under the control of managers. In the 1960s, work motivation theories entered into its golden age and procured a flurry of new theoretical perspectives (for reviews, see Ambrose & Kulik, 1999; Greenberg & Colquitt,

2005; Latham & Pinder, 2005; Locke & Latham, 2002; Van Eerde & Thierry, 1996). Although these perspectives emphasized the importance of employees' intentions, motives and desires, they still held the assumption that employees could only evaluate passively and select among the reinforcement contingencies that provided by managers. For example, needs theories demonstrated that individuals were motivated by managers to engage in behaviors that resulted in the satisfaction of personal needs (Maslow, 1954; McClelland, 1961, 1971). Goal-setting theory assumed that specific and challenging goals set by managers increased employees' performance (Locke, 1968). Equity theory predicted that employees adjusted their behaviors according to the fairness of outcomes and rewards from managers and organizations (Adams, 1963, 1965). Moreover, expectancy theory stated that individuals tended to engage in behaviors based on the expectation that the behaviors would be followed by a given outcome and on the attractiveness of the outcome (Vroom, 1964).

However, in the 1970s and 1980s, this central assumption started to receive some challenges from organizational scholars working in diverse research fields, such as in the influence and feedback literatures. Specifically, in the influence research, researchers have emphasized that employees actively utilize tactics to influence others around them (Kipnis, Schmidt & Wilkinson, 1980; Williams, Gray & von Broembsen, 1976). In the feedback literature, researchers recognized that employees actively monitored work environment and sought feedback pertaining to organizational or personal goals rather than sat and waited for feedback from supervisors (Ashford & Cummings, 1983, 1985).

More recently, researchers studying diverse organizational topics have emphasized the active role that employees could play in the workplace. For example, in studying job design, researchers have observed that employees not only adjust to jobs that are structured by managers, but also actively change their job characteristics and bargain for favorable work conditions with managers (Ilgen & Hollenbeck, 1991). Researchers studying organizational learning behaviors have shown that employees do not only passively expand their knowledge and skills by request; they actively search for learning opportunities and engage in learning activities (Edmondson, 1999; Sonnentag, 2003). Similarly, in the citizenship literature, researchers have shifted the focus of reactive behaviors toward more proactive actions including offering help and consciously breaking rules (Morrison, 2006; Rioux & Penner, 2001).

Taken together, these research streams show that employees are proactive and active when changing their environments.

2.2 Definition of Proactive Behavior

Whilst developing these diverse proactive concepts in separate literatures, researchers have sought to take an integrative view of proactivity recently. The first relevant view focuses on proactive personality, which is defined as "a dispositional construct that identifies differences among people in the extent to which they take action to influence their environments" (Bateman & Crant, 1993). Based on this conceptualization, considerable empirical studies have focused on the topic of proactive personality and related it to various work outcomes (e.g., Crant & Bateman, 2000; Fuller & Marler, 2009; Gong, Cheung, Wang & Huang, 2012; Seibert, Kraimer & Crant, 2001). Although Bateman and Crant initially described proactive behaviors to be change-oriented, their dispositional perspective did not provide so much information about what behaviors could be viewed as proactive (Crant, 2000).

A more relevant concept of proactive behavior is personal initiative, defined as "a behavior syndrome resulting in an individual's taking an active and self-starting approach to work and going beyond what is formally required in a given job" (Frese, Kring, Soose & Zempel, 1996). From this definition, personal initiative has several characteristics: it (1) is self-starting, (2) is anticipatory and forward-looking, (3) is consistent with the organization's goals and (4) includes only pro-organizational actions (Grant & Ashford, 2008). Therefore, personal initiative only captures part of individual proactivity, and excludes those pro-self or anti-organizational proactive actions (Ashford, Blatt & Vande Walle, 2003; Griffin & Lopez, 2005).

Incombination with the above two concepts, scholars have continuously refined the definition of proactive behavior from the integrative perspective. Several definitions of employee proactive behavior are illustrated in Table 2.1. These definitions consistently identify several key elements. First, proactive behavior is anticipatory. Employees are anticipating, envisioning, planning, and acting in advance (Frese & Fay, 2001; Parker & Collins, 2010). Second, proactive behavior has intended impact. The purpose of initiating change is to make a difference (Grant, 2007) and to improve the situation or oneself (Grant & Ashford, 2008). Third, proactive behavior is self-initiated. Employees could engage in proactive actions without being told or without an explicit requirement in the formal job description (Parker et al., 2006). In this study, I employed Grant and Ashford's (2008) definition which captured the above-mentioned three characteristics well.

TABLE 2.1 Definitions of Proactive Behavior

Articles	Definition
Crant (2000)	taking initiative in improving current circumstances; it involves challenging the status quo rather than passively adapting present conditions (p. 436)
Unsworth & Parker (2003)	a set of self-starting, action-oriented behaviors aimed at modifying the situation or oneself to achieve greater personal or organizational effectiveness (p. 180)
Parker, Williams & Turner (2006)	self-initiated and future-oriented action that aims to change and improve the situation oroneself (p. 636)

续表

Articles	Definition
Griffin, Neal & Parker (2007)	self-directed action to anticipate or initiate change in the work system or work roles (p. 329)
Grant & Ashford (2008)	anticipatory action that employees take to impact themselves and/or their environments (p. 8)

In organizational studies, the concept of organizational citizenship behavior is quite similar to proactive behavior. Organ (1990) defines organizational citizenship behavior as behaviors that go above and beyond the specified requirements of the job. It is also called as extra-role behaviors. The definitions show that these two kinds of behaviors share a common characteristic, namely discretionary and self-initiated. Thus, researchers have difficulties differentiating these two behaviors. However, more recent work suggests that a more appropriate way is to classify employees' activities, including task, conceptual, extra-role, and citizenship behaviors with different degrees of proactivity (Bindl & Parker, 2011; Parker et al., 2006). It seems that there is no need to confine proactive behaviors to the citizenship domain only.

2.3 Type of Proactive Behavior

Driven by the importance of the phenomenon, organizational researchers have investigated a wide range of proactive concepts, which vary in terms of the type of behavior exhibited. An illustrative list includes taking initiative (Frese et al., 1996), expressing voice (Le Pine & Van Dyne, 1998), taking charge to improve work methods and procedures (Morrison & Phelps, 1999), proactive problem prevention (Parker et al., 2006), building networks (Morrison,

2002), career initiative actions (Seibert et al., 2001), and proactive service performance (Rank, Carsten, Unger & Spector, 2007). Although these constructs are all generally self-initiated and future-focused, they are different from one another. Using taking charge and voice as examples, taking charge is more behavioral than voice. Much of earlier literature focused on just one type of behavior. However, there are limitations in these studies because not much is known about whether these various concepts are related and general antecedents and processes of proactive behaviors exist or not (Parker & Collins, 2010).

Therefore, recently, an increasing number of studies have started to examine more than one type of proactive behaviors. For example, Parker and Collins (2010) first used a sample of 622 managers and found that various proactive concepts were distinct from each other but related through a higher-order structure. Using a subsample of 319 managers, they also reported similarities and differences in the antecedents of the proactive concepts. Specifically, proactive work behavior included taking charge, voice, individual innovation, and problem prevention. Proactive personality, role breadth self-efficacy, and felt responsibility for change were consistently positive antecedents; learning goal orientation positively related to all of these work role behaviors except for voice; and performance goal orientation was a consistent negative antecedent for all excluding proactive problem prevention. Proactive strategic behavior included issue selling and strategic scanning. Consideration of future consequences and performance goal orientation were consistent predictors but learning goal orientation was not. Finally, proactive person-environment fit behavior included feedback inquiry, feedback monitoring, job change negotiation, and career initiative. Conscientiousness positively related to all of these person-environment behaviors except for career initiative.

Other researchers have examined the influence of antecedents on different types of proactive behaviors in two studies to test the generalizability of the findings. For instance, Den Hartog and Belschak (2012) argued that personal initiative and prosocial proactive behavior (proactive behavior targeted at the organization or colleagues) were highly correlated with each other, and investigated the effect of a three-way interaction of transformational leadership, role-breadth self-efficacy and job autonomy on employee proactive behavior in two studies. Their results showed that when autonomy was high, transformational leadership related positively to proactive behavior for individuals high (but not low) on RBSE. On the contrary, when job autonomy was low, transformational leadership related positively to proactive behavior for individuals low (but not high) on self-efficacy. This pattern was found for both employees' personal initiative in Study 1 and employees' prosocial proactive behavior in Study 2.

A more recent study by Lam, Spreitzer and Fritz (2013) used a similar research design and tested the curvilinear effect of positive affect on both voice in a sample of 236 knowledge workers and general proactive behaviors in a sample of 196 service workers. Findings from these two studies indicated that intermediate levels of positive affect were most beneficial for employees' proactive behaviors. In line with these studies, this study focuses on personal initiative in Study 1 and three foci of proactive behaviors in Study 2.

2.4　Target of Proactive Behavior

Proactive behavior can vary with respect to intended target of form—whom the behavior is intended to impact. Researchers indicated that employees could simultaneously direct their proactive behavior toward three primary targets: the self, other people and the organization as a whole (Grant & Ashford, 2008; Van Dyne, Cummings & McLean Parks, 1995). Several representative studies on employee proactive behavior toward different targets are listed in Table 2.2.

TABLE 2.2 Studies on Employee Proactive Behavior toward Different Targets

Articles	Foci of proactive behavior	Targets
Griffin, Neal & Parker (2007)	Individual task proactivity, team member proactivity, organization member proactivity	The organization, coworkers, self
Strauss, Griffin & Rafferty (2009)	Team member proactivity, organization member proactivity	The organization, coworkers
Parker & Collins (2010)	Proactive work behavior, proactive strategic behavior, proactive person–environment fit behavior	The organization, self
Belschak & Den Hartog (2010)	Pro-organizational proactive behavior, prosocial proactive behavior, pro-self proactive behavior	The organization, coworkers, self
Liu, Zhu & Yang (2010)	Speaking up, speaking out	The supervisor, coworkers
Liu, Tangirala & Ramanujam (2013)	Speaking up to the direct leader, speaking up to the skip-level leader	The supervisor, supervisor's boss

Griffin et al. (2007) was the first to identify three foci of proactivity. Specifically, individual task proactivity refers to behaviors that are required and expected by an employee's role as an individual (e.g., improving ways of doing tasks), team member proactivity reflects behaviors that are required and expected by an individual's role as a member of a team (e.g., making improvements to team work methods), and organization member proactivity refers to actions that are required and expected by an individual's role as a member of an organization (e.g., making suggestions to improve the overall effectiveness of the organization).

In their empirical study, Parker and Collins (2010) followed the intended target of impact and distinguished the multiple forms of self-initiated and change-oriented behaviors into three higher – order categories. First, proactive work behavior is directed at improving the internal organization environment. For instance, employees can often develop and make recommendations about issues that affect their work unit (Van Dyne & Le Pine, 1998). Second, proactive strategic behavior is directed at improving the organization's fit with the external environment. Examples include strategic scanning of the environment, influencing the formation of a strategy in an organization by making others aware of particular issues, and influencing the formation of a strategy in an organization by giving resources. Third, proactive person – environment fit behavior is directed at improving the individual's fit within the organizational environment. For example, individuals can promote their careers actively rather than respond to the job situation passively.

Following the suggestions made by Grant and Ashford (2008), Belschak and Den Hartog (2010) suggested three foci of proactive behavior and empirically examined the antecedents of these behaviors. More specifically, pro-organizational proactive behavior describes anticipatory actions that employees take to affect or change the organization; prosocial proactive behavior describes those behaviors aimed at changing the workgroup; and pro – self proactive behavior includes actions that employees take to facilitate the achievement of personal goals. Finally, Liu et al. focused mainly on a type of organizational proactive behavior—voice and differentiated speaking up to supervisor, speaking out to coworkers, and speaking up to skip-level supervisor (Liu et al., 2010, 2013).

Taken together, in this study, I argue that supervisor is another important target when employees perform proactive behavior and supervisory abuse will have an impact not only on general proactive behavior, but also on proactive behaviors that are directed at the organization, supervisor and coworkers.

2.5 Antecedents of Employee Proactive Behavior

In my review of the predictors of proactive behavior, I classified the findings into two major groups: situational factors and individual differences, which follow.

2.5.1 Situational Antecedents

Generally speaking, previous research has demonstrated three key categories of contextual antecedents of proactive behavior. The first category is about job design. Job characteristics literature has shown that job conditions enhance perceptions of control and capability, therefore influence the levels of proactivity (Parker et al., 2010). In this vein, job conditions such as job autonomy, complexity and control, all pertaining to the controllability an individual could have in his or her job, have been consistently found to be positively associated with proactive behaviors (Parker et al., 2006; Frese, Garst & Fay, 2007). For example, job autonomy has been found to be positively associated with proactive behaviors in terms of personal initiative, idea implementation and problem solving (Hornung & Rousseau, 2007, Parker et al., 2006). Likewise, job control, together with other job resources such as variety and feedback, has been shown to predict personal initiative (Hakanen, Perhoniemi & Toppinen-Tanner, 2008; Salanova & Schaufeli, 2008).

Moreover, negative job characteristics, or job stressors have been argued to influence proactive behavior. Conceptually, challenge stressors such as time pressure and situational constraints could be positively related to proactive behavior because these factors could be perceived by individuals as the difference between a desired and an actual situation, thus motivating them to actively shorten such difference and enhance their personal initiative (Carver & Scheier, 1982; Frese & Fay, 2001) Empirically, based on four waves of a longitudinal study with 172 to 193 individuals, Fay and Sonnentag (2002) showed that time pressure and situational constraints had positive effects on personal initiative. Using a randomly selected sample of 278 employees, Ohly, Sonnentag and Pluntke (2006) found that time pressure had a positive relationship with proactive behavior. Consistently, Ohly and Fritz (2010) in a multi-level study reported that time pressure was perceived as challenging, and thus increased the level of proactive work behavior.

On the other hand, hindrance stressors such as role ambiguity and role conflict could play a role in affecting proactive behavior. Fuller et al. (2006) theorized that individuals with high levels of role ambiguity were uncertain about how to contribute to organizational performance and about how to make constructive changes that help achieve organizational objectives. However, using a sample of 115 employees from a small utility company, they failed to find support for their arguments. Using individual innovative performance as the measurement of proactive behavior, the results were also divergent. For example, Ivancevich and Donnelly (1974) reported a positive relationship between role clarity and perceived opportunity for innovation. Other researchers such as Spreitzer (1995) and Leung, Huang, Su and Lu (2011) revealed a nonsignificant or even curvilinear relationship between role stress and innovative performance.

The second relevant situational factor is supervisory leadership, as supervisors may influence subordinates' proactive actions by impacting their work motivations and environments. As shown in Appendix A, I conducted a systematic review of empirical studies on the supervisory antecedents and individual-level proactivity. Supervisory transformational leadership, leading by motivating followers to commit to organizational goals and realize performance outcomes that go beyond expectations, has received most attention in the proactivity research. It has been found to enhance followers' identification with the group or the leader (Liu et al., 2010), perceived psychological safety (Detert & Burris, 2007), and perceived capabilities of being proactive (Strauss et al., 2009) and thus predict different forms of proactivity in terms of innovative behaviors (Pieterse, Van Knippenberg, Schippers & Stam, 2010; Rank et al., 2009), taking charge (Li, Chiaburu, Kirkman & Xie, 2013), as well as voice behavior (Detert & Burris, 2007). Transformational leadership has also been shown to simultaneously influence employee proactivity toward two or more targets. Specifically, Liu and colleagues (2010) showed that transformational leadership simultaneously predicted speaking up to supervisor and speaking out to coworkers. Likewise, Belschak and Den Hartog (2010) indicated that transformational leadership was an important predictor for pro-organizational, pro-social and pro-self proactive behaviors.

The second type of supervisory factors that gained much attention is supervisor support or leader-member exchange (LMX). Supervisor support may enhance subordinates' feelings of self-determination and being valued by the organization, thereby resulting in high levels of personal initiative (Ohly, Sonnentag & Pluntke, 2006). Other researchers argued that special support from supervisors such as encouraging self-observation and self-goal setting might promote proactive idea implementation and problem prevention (Parker et al., 2006). LMX, a similar concept of supervisor support, has also been suggested to influence employees' proactivity. LMX refers to the relationship quality between employees and supervisors (Liden, Sparrowe & Wayne, 1997). The quality of interactions with supervisors can impact psychological detachment from the employing organization (Burris et al., 2006), and form fondness, loyalty and respect for each other (Zhang, Huai & Xie, 2014). As a consequence, it encourages individuals to exhibit self-initiated and future-focused behaviors. Empirically, LMX has been found to have a positive relationship with specific proactive behaviors in terms of innovative job performance (Janssen & Van Yperen, 2004; Scott & Bruce, 1994; Yuan & Woodman, 2010), speaking up (Burris et al., 2008; Liu et al., 2013; Zhang et al., 2014), as well as negative feedback-seeking behaviors (Chen, Lam & Zhong, 2007).

Recently, other types of supervisory leadership have also been explored in the proactivity research. Supervisory ethical leadership refers to "the demonstration of normatively appropriate conduct through personal actions and interpersonal relationships, and the promotion of such conduct to followers through two - way communication, reinforcement, and decision - making" (Brown, Treviño & Harrison, 2005, p. 120). Ethical supervisors publicly criticized inappropriate actions, emphasized doing the right thing, and became a role model for followers to emulate. Therefore, subordinates were more likely to speak out constructive ideas (Avey et al., 2012; Walumbwa & Schaubroeck, 2009; Yang & Liu, 2014).

A limited number of studies noticed the importance of destructive supervision and examined its role in affecting subordinates' proactive behaviors. For instance, Ng and Feldman (2012) argued that supervisor undermining–actions that hindered subordinates' abilities to establish positive interpersonal relationships, depleted subordinates' emotional energy and resources, resulting in low levels of innovation-related behaviors. They collected data from 196 employees at three times over one year, and found support for the aforementioned hypothesis. Burris et al. (2008) found that abusive supervision increased subordinates' intentions to quit, and then undermined their voice behaviors toward the supervisor.

Additionally, skip-level leader (i.e., supervisor's boss) variables could have an effect on followers' initiative behaviors. For example, Morrison and Phelps (1999) collected both self-report and coworker data for 275 white-collar employees from various companies, and found that top managements' openness to change predicted employees' willingness to engage in taking charge behaviors. Using a sample of 3149 employees and 223 managers in a restaurant chain, Detert and Burris (2007) revealed that general managers' transformational leadership behaviors and openness were significantly and negatively linked to subordinate improvement-oriented voice. In addition, building on the socially embedded nature of leader-member exchanges, Liu et al. (2013) used a sample of 237 employees and their direct and skip-level leaders, and found that the linkage between voice to the direct leader and the exchange quality between the employee and the direct leader was more positive when the exchange relationship between the direct leader and the skip-level leader was stronger.

The final type of situational antecedents is about interpersonal climate and social processes. Proactive behavior is an interpersonal action so that it is likely to be impacted by other individuals' reactions in the workplace. Coworkers' support for proactive actions can influence individuals' capability and motivation, and thus, lead to high levels of proactive behaviors. On the other hand, poor relationships can make the costs of performing proactive behaviors too high. Empirically, individuals who have trust in coworkers' abilities, and are supported by team members are more likely to engage in specific forms of proactive behavior such as issue selling behaviors (Ashford, Rothbard, Piderit & Dutton, 1998) and job search behavior (Kanfer, Wanberg & Kantrowitz, 2001), and general forms of proactive behavior such as proactive idea implementation and problem solving (Parker et al., 2006), taking charge (Love & Dustin, 2014), voice (Le Pine & Van Dyne, 1998) as well as team member proactivity (Griffin et al., 2007).

Organizational climates and norms have received relatively little attention in the proactivity literature. Some researchers argued that norms supporting risk taking or issue selling could encourage issue selling and taking charge behaviors (Ashford et al., 1998; Morrison & Phelps, 1999). Other researchers focused on climate for proactivity and initiative. For instance, Baer and Frese (2003) referred to climate for initiative as "formal and informal organizational practices and procedures guiding and supporting a proactive, self-starting, and persistent approach toward work" (p. 48). Later, Raub and Liao (2012) refined this definition and measurement, and indicated that initiative climate had a positive relationship with proactive customer service performance. In a related vein, scholars conceptualized voice climate and also found that voice climate was strongly and positively related to voice (Frazier & Bowler, 2012; Morrison, Wheeler-Smith & Kamdar, 2011).

2.5.2 Individual Antecedents

Consistent with pastreviews (Bindl & Parker, 2011; Parker et al., 2010), individual differences contain personality, knowledge, skills and abilities, positive affectivity as well as demographics.

There has been substantial interest in the influence of personality on different proactive concepts. Proactive personality, the most frequently explored trait, is highly relevant for multiple types of proactive behaviors because of its change-oriented and self-initiated focus. Consistently, proactive personality has been found to predict voice behavior, taking charge to improve work processes and career initiative (for a review, see Fuller & Marler, 2009). Other empirical studies have also shown that proactive personality has its impacts via several motivational processes. For example, Parker and colleagues (2006) found that proactive personality could increase a person's perceived capability of carrying our proactive activities, and sense of personal responsibility for a broader range of goals, and in turn, resulted in higher levels of proactive idea implementation and problem prevention.

Other relevant personality dimensions are conscientiousness, goal orientation, and intellectual curiosity. Conscientiousness, or the tendency of an individual to be hardworking, resourceful, and dependable as well as be thorough, was consistently linked to various proactive behaviors unlike other big-5 personality dimensions. For example, Conscientiousness predicted proactive job search (Kanfer et al., 2001), career planning behaviors (Carless & Bernath, 2007), and proactive person - environment fit behaviors (Parker & Collins, 2010).

Learning goal orientation, reflecting a preference to understand or master new aspects, has been found to predict feedback seeking behaviors (Tuckey, Brewer & Williamson, 2002), taking charge to improve work procedures, and individual innovative behaviors (Parker & Collins, 2010).

Knowledge, skills and abilities have also been shown to affect individuals' proactive behaviors. For instance, Dutton, Ashford, O'Neill and Lawrence (2001) reported that three facets of knowledge enhanced individuals' proactive issue selling actions to the top management. Similarly, Howell and Boies (2004) indicated that contextual knowledge was positively linked to employees' framing of ideas for promotion. Further, education is a critical antecedent for proactivity. For example, for a sample of 441 full-time employees in 95 work groups, educational background predicted speaking out with improvement suggestions (Le Pine & Van Dyne, 1998). Likewise, in a study with employees in East Germany, the authors found support for a positive relationship between cognitive ability and personal initiative (Fay & Frese, 2001).

Another type of individual antecedents is trait affectivity, which has gained increasing attention in proactivity literature. Trait affectivity is defined as a tendency to feel consistently across time and situations (Parkinson, Totterdell, Briner & Reynolds, 1996). An individual high in positive affectivity tends to feel excited, joyful, enthusiastic, and active (Watson, Clark & Tellegen, 1988). As suggested by Parker and colleagues (2010), positive affectivity could influence an individual's capability of being proactive, as well as the level of intrinsic motivation, and finally, led to proactive work behaviors. Empirically, Den Hartog and Belschak (2007) indicated that trait positive affectivity enhanced proactive actions such as taking initiative and suggesting improvements. Using a sample of ninety-two individuals, Madrid, Patterson, Birdi, Leiva and Kausel (2014) reported a positive effect of positive affectivity on innovative work behaviors. Negative affectivity has been linked to individuals' higher levels of negative affective experiences (Bindl & Parker, 2012) and has nonconsistent effects on proactive behaviors. For example, Venkataramani and Tangirala (2010) conducted a study using a sample of 184 bank employees, and found that negative affectivity was negatively related to voice. But in Lam et al.'s (2013) study, negative affectivity was not significantly associated with proactive behaviors.

Demographics including age, gender and ethnicity have also been suggested to influence individuals' engagement in proactive behaviors. However, the extant empirical results are inconsistent and inconclusive. For example, some studies found no relationships between age and proactive behavior (Morrison & Phelps, 1999) whereas others showed a negative relationship with age (Jannsen & Van Yperen, 2004) and one study suggested more proactivity with age (Warr & Fay, 2001). Moreover, Griffin and colleagues (2007) found inconsistent results for the relationship between gender and proactivity. For ethnicity, Le Pine and Van Dyne (1998) showed that white employees were more likely to voice concerns, on the other hand, Kanfer and colleagues (2001) found that white employees were less likely to proactively search jobs. In sum, relatively little research has explored the association between demographics and proactive behaviors.

2.6 Motivational Processes

To fully understand the relationships between antecedents and proactive behaviors, I discuss the underlying motivational processes. Specifically, I report the evidence according to a review by Parker et al. (2010). They identified three motivational processes: a "can do" motivation that referred to perceived capability of performing proactive behaviors, a "reason to" motivation that represented an individual's desire to engage in proactive behaviors, and an "energized to" motivation that reflected the individual's moods or emotions to be proactive. This classification of the motivational processes is echoed by a number of researchers (Bindl & Parker, 2011; Fuller, Marler & Hester, 2012; Raub & Liao, 2012).

2.6.1 "Can Do" Motivational Process

Turning to the first motivational state, as suggested by Parker et al. (2006), when a person acts proactively, he or she will ask questions such as Can I do it? How risky is it? Or how feasible is it? Therefore, this type of motivation draws on theories that focus on expectancy, including social-cognitive theory (Bandura, 1982), action theory (Hacker, 1985), expectancy theory (Vroom, 1964) and job characteristics theory (Hackman & Oldham, 1976).

Self-efficacy, defined as a belief that one can exercise some control over his or her own functioning (Bandura, 1997), has been viewed as the most important mechanism in the proactivity literature. For example, drawing from self-efficacy theory, general self-efficacy can raise an individual's feeling of control and perceived opportunities of success, and thus is positively related to proactive behaviors like initiative (Speier & Frese, 1997), proactive customer service performance (Raub & Liao, 2012) and taking charge (Morrison & Phelps, 1999). In addition, specific domains of self-efficacy have also been investigated in proactivity literature. Role breadth self-efficacy refers to one's perceived capability to carry out a range of proactive, interpersonal, and integrative tasks that go beyond the prescribed technical core (Parker et al., 2006). It has been shown to predict improvement suggestions (Axtell, Holman, Unsworth, Wall & Waterson, 2000), personal initiative (Ohly & Fritz, 2007); voice and taking charge (Parker & Collins, 2010). In a study of 2155 employees from two organizations, Griffin and colleagues (2007) found that role-breadth self-efficacy was simultaneously associated with indicial task proactivity, team member proactivity and organization member proactivity. Moreover, Strauss et al. (2009) reported that role breadth self-efficacy mediated the relationship between team leader transformational leadership and team member proactivity.

The perceived cost of behavior, or the negative consequences of performing the tasks, is also suggested to be a process underpinning proactive behavior. For example, based on a study of 216 employees from a wide range of jobs, Yuan and Woodman (2010) employed expectancy theory, and indicated that expected image risks mediated the relationships between perceived organization support for innovation, innovativeness as a job requirement and individual innovative behavior. Similarly, in a sample of 952 graduates from a Midwestern business school, Ashford et al. (1998) found that perceived image risks mediated the relationships between context favorability (perceived organizational support, norms favoring issue selling and relationship quality) and issue selling willingness.

A third motivational state is control appraisal, an individual's belief that they will control the situation. Individuals with high control appraisals tend to maintain a strong sense of responsibility, be persistent through difficulties, and actively search for information and opportunities, thereby promoting favorable work outcomes (Frese & Fay, 2001). Parker et al. (2006) suggested that control appraisal worked as a mediator in the relationship between supervisor support and proactive work behavior. Frese, Garst and Fay (2007) in their longitudinal study found that control appraisal worked as a mediator in the relationship between work characteristics and personal initiative.

2.6.2 "Reason To" Motivational Process

Turning to the second motivational state, people may have a strong reason to be proactive. In other words, they will ask themselves questions such as Why should I engage in this behavior? Do I want to do this? Why should I perform this behavior? This "reason to" motivation therefore maps onto theories such as self-determination theory (Deci & Ryan, 2000) and flow theory (Csikszentmihalyi,

1988).

Several psychological factors have been identified as "reason to" motivations. The first factor is flexible role orientation. Individuals with flexible role orientations define their personal responsibilities broadly and experience a strong sense of ownership of goals and problems beyond their immediate set of tasks, considering them as "my job" rather than as "someone else's job" (Parker, Wall & Jackson, 1997). Empirically, Ohly and Fritz (2007) in a sample of 98 employees and coworkers, found a positive relationship between role orientation and personal initiative. In addition, based on a sample of 282 U. K. wire makers, Parker et al. (2006) found support for the assumptions that employees' flexible role orientation mediated the associations between antecedents (proactive personality, job autonomy and coworker trust) and proactive work behavior.

Second, felt responsibility for constructive change, or one's feeling of being personally obligated to bring about constructive change, has been found to be related to various proactive concepts conceptually and empirically. For instance, Morrison and Phelps (1999) found that an employee who felt a high responsibility for change would perceive a strong sense of satisfaction and accomplishment, and was more likely to exhibit challenging behaviors. Researchers have found similar results for the relationships with promotive voice (Liang, Farh & Farh, 2012) and with taking charge (Fuller et al., 2012). More importantly, Fuller et al. (2006) reported that felt responsibility for constructive change was as a key process linking work design characteristics (e. g., positive in organization hierarchy and access to resources) to voice behavior. Choi (2007) also indicated that felt responsibility for change mediated the association between innovative climate and proactive behaviors in terms of taking charge and innovative behavior.

The third motivational construct of proactivity isorganizational identification, "a perceived oneness with an organization and the experience of the organization's successes and failures as one's own" (Mael & Ashforth, 1992, p. 103). Empirical evidence showed that individuals with organizational identification were more likely to exhibit high levels of proactive behavior (Morrison et al., 2011) and that this motivation mediated the relationships between transformational leadership, ethical leadership and individual voice behaviors (Liu et al., 2010; Yang & Liu, 2014).

2.6.3 "Energized To" Motivational Process

In addition to the "can do" and "reason to" motivational states, individual proactive behavior may be influenced by "hot" affective motivational state. When one performs such behavior, he or she will ask: Am I happy to do this? Thus, this motivation is drawn on the broaden-and-build theory of positive emotions (Fredrickson, 1998, 2001), and the circumplex model of affect (Russell, 2003).

Work engagement, the positive work-related affect, reflects an individual's feelings of work-related vigor, dedication and absorption (Maslach, Schaufeli & Leiter, 2001). Drawing from the broaden-and-build model of positive emotions, employees who feel engaged in their work are more likely to engage in future-focused behaviors that aim to change the situation or themselves, than those who feel less engaged. In support of this, Salanova and Schaufeli (2008) indicated that, in two different samples, work engagement mediated the relationship between job resources and personal initiative. In a longitudinal study, Hakanen and colleagues (2008) found that job resources predicted personal initiative via work engagement. Further support for the mediating role of work engagement stemmed from a diary study. Sonnentag (2003) reported that day-level work engagement mediated the relationships between recovery and day-level self-initiative, as well as the pursuit of learning.

Other researchers have found that positive moods are the key mediating processes linking situations to individual proactive behaviors. For example, Hsiung (2012), using a multi-level data from 70 workgroups of a Taiwan company, built a model based on the broaden-and-built model of positive moods and found support for the mediating role of positive moods in the relationship between authentic leadership and employee voice behavior. More recently, Madrid et al. (2014) argued that support for innovation could spark positive feelings high in activation because innovative work required valuable psychological resources including mastery, and collaboration, and that high-activated positive moods could enhance innovative behavior by broadening thinking and resulting in flexible cognition. They tested this model using data from 92 individuals from 73 different companies, and found support for the hypotheses.

2.7 Boundary Conditions

Proactivity researchers have adopted an interactional perspective, and examined the interplay of situational and individual antecedents. For instance, drawing on behavior plasticity theory (Brockner, 1988), Le Pine and Van Dyne (1998) found that favorable situational factors (e.g., high levels of overall group autonomy) were more strongly and positively related to voice behaviors in a work group for individuals with lower levels of self-esteem than for individuals with higher levels of self-esteem. In a similar vein, Speier and Frese (1997) found that the relationship between job control and personal initiative was stronger for those individuals with low levels of generalized self-efficacy beliefs. Using a sample of 586 nurses, Tangirala and Ramanujam (2008) found support for the moderating role of organizational identification in the personal control-voice link. By the same token, Jassen and Gao (2013) found support for the assumption that the relationship between supervisory responsiveness and voice was stronger when subordinates were high in voice self-efficacy.

Researchers have also found that the effect of individual difference on self-initiated behaviors is contingent. For example, Premeaux and Bedeian (2003) argued that low self-monitors spoke up more often as top management openness and trust in supervisor increased. Using a sample of telecommunications employees, they found support for the above argument. A study by Grant and Sumanth (2009), using a sample of professional fundraisers working for a US-based university, found that individuals with high dispositional trust propensity were more likely to be motivated to show high-levels of initiative even when their managers were not trustworthy. Similarly, in a multi-source study, Wu, Parker and De Jong (2011) found that the relationship between need for cognition and innovation behavior was strongest for individuals who have low job autonomy and low time pressure, and this relationship was nonsignificant at high levels of these situational variables. Furthermore, Raub and Liao (2012) drew from synergistic person-situation theory (Pervin, 1989) and found support for the argument that initiative climate magnified the relationship between general self-efficacy and proactive customer service performance.

2.8 Consequences of Employee Proactive Behavior

Except for the predictors, empirical studies have also investigated the outcomes of individual proactive behaviors and reported that they were positively related to job performance, job satisfaction, career satisfaction, turnover and other favorable outcomes (for reviews, see Bindl & Parker, 2011; Thomas, Whitman & Viswesvaran, 2010).

Proactive behavior has been linked to superior job performance. Proactive individuals may study their situations in a rigorous manner, and form environments that enhance the levels of performance (Seibert et al., 1999). Proactive employees may also actively customize their situations in a way that complement their strengths and increase the likelihood of high levels of performance (Crant, 2000). Empirically, in their review, Thomas et al. (2010) indicated that personal initiative, voice, and taking charge were positively related to overall performance. Belschak and Den Hartog (2010) who conducted a study using 126 employee-peer dyads found that organizational and personal proactive behaviors were positively associated with individual task performance. Similarly, in a longitudinal study, Van Dyne and Le Pine (1998) indicated employees exhibiting high levels of voice were rated by supervisors as better performers six months later. Further, based on a two-wave 3-year longitudinal study of 2555 Finnish dentists, Hakanen et al. (2008) found that personal initiative was a powerful predictor of work-unit innovativeness.

Job attitudes are another type of dependent variables. It might be that proactive employees were able to remove obstacles in the organization, experience a sense of autonomy and task significance, and gain career success. For example, in a study of 181 newcomers, Wanberg and Kammeyer-Mueller (2000) found that proactive relationship building had strong relationships with job satisfaction and intention to turnover. In a similar string of research, Seibert et al. (2001) in their 2-year longitudinal study indicated that employees who exhibited high levels of innovative behaviors and career initiative were more likely to report high levels of career satisfaction. Moreover, employees who showed voice behavior might facilitate a high-quality leader-member exchange relationship, resulting in higher levels of work engagement (Cheng, Lu, Chang & Johnstone, 2012) and higher levels of organizational affective commitment (Farndale, Van Ruiten, Kelliher & Hope-Hailey, 2011). In their conceptual paper, Spitzmuller and Van Dyne (2013) also argued that proactive helping might facilitate positive moods, self-esteem, need satisfaction and self-development.

Moreover, employees may achieve other benefits by exhibiting proactive actions. Specifically, employees who engage in personal initiative have been found to be more likely to enhance work control and complexity (Frese et al., 2007), gain anticipated benefits (Hornung & Rousseau, 2007) and devise, ask for and negotiate working conditions that are beneficial for themselves and their employing organizations (Hornung, Rousseau & Glaser, 2008). Another type of proactivity, innovative behavior is positively associated with salary progression and promotions in past 2 years (Seibert et al., 2001).

Taking everything together, prior research on employee proactivity has mainly investigated the antecedents, motivational processes, boundary conditions and outcomes. The overall framework of employee proactivity is provided in Figure 2.1.

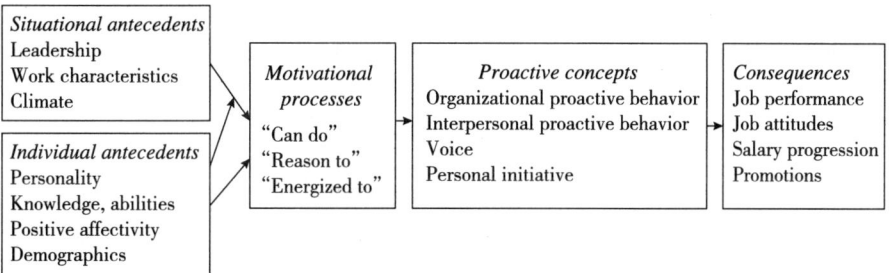

FIGURE 2.1 Framework of Employee Proactive Behavior

2.9 Emerging Issues in Proactive Behavior Research

After reviewing the literature, I discover some research issues pertaining to proactivity. These issues cover the role of abusive supervision and potential moderators.

2.9.1 Role of Abusive Supervision

Although researchers have made great strides in investigating the influential factors of individual proactivity, most of such research has focused on job characteristics and positive leader and supervisor behaviors (e. g., Frese, Teng & Wijnen, 1999; Ohly et al., 2006; Parker et al., 2006). Yet in organizational life, supervisors can act destructively, and become rude or even scornful to employees (Tepper, 2000). The impact of such supervisory abuse cannot be directly inferred from research findings on positive supervisory actions. Moreover, Parker et al. (2010) called for more research on examining the effects of social factors (i. e., supervisory behaviors). As argued by Grant and Ashford (2008), "considerable research is needed to examine a broader range of situational influences on proactivity" (p. 22). Therefore, it is necessary to further investigate the relationships between destructive supervisory actions and subordinate proactive behaviors.

According to my previous review, thus far, there have been five studies examining the influence of destructive supervisory behaviors on individuals' proactive behaviors. Specifically, Burris et al. (2008) found support for the relationship between abusive supervision and proactive behavior in terms of voice to the supervisor and such relationship was mediated by intention to leave. Li et al. (2009) used a sample of 504 Chinese employees and confirmed that abusive supervision's negative effect on promotive voice was mediated by perceived organizational support (POS), and its negative effect on prohibitive voice was mediated by POS and psychological safety and abusive supervision was more strongly associated with POS when subordinates perceived higher supervisory status. In a related vein, Rafferty and Restubog (2011) reported that abusive supervision was negatively linked to followers' perceptions of interactional justice, which in turn led to supervisor-rated prosocial voice behaviors.

Further, Kammeyer-Mueller, Wanberg, Rubenstein and Song (2013) conducted a 14-wave longitudinal study with a sample of 264 organizational newcomers, but failed to find a significant association between supervisor undermining (similar to abusive supervision, Tepper, 2007) and individual organizational proactivity. Likewise, Ng and Feldman (2012) collected data from 196 employees at three points in time and reported a nonsignificant relationship between supervisor undermining and individual innovation.

Several questions remain unanswered from these studies. First, three of the five studies have chosen voice as the dependent variable and one study has focused on individual innovation. Voice is viewed as one type of proactivity, and focuses on suggestion-making which is more vocal. Individual innovation is also one form of proactivity and emphasizes novelty; therefore, it is difficult to generalize these findings to other types of proactive behavior beyond voice (Lam et al., 2013). Second, these studies have mainly utilized social exchange perspective to explain the mechanism linking destructive supervision to proactive concepts. Abusive supervision literature has widely viewed supervisory abuse as a workplace stressor, thereby making a stress perspective appropriate for understanding the occurrence of proactive behavior. Such perspective has been emphasized by some researchers such as Fay and Grant (e.g., Frese & Fay, 2001; Grant & Rothbard, 2013), but still needs more scholarly attention (e.g., Grant & Ashford, 2008; Ohly & Fritz, 2010). Third, the findings on the associations between abusive supervision and proactive concepts from the five studies are not consistent. Moreover, depending on individual difference and situations, followers' reactions to destructive supervision are not always negative (Tepper, 2007). Thus, this study also examines the boundary conditions, or potential moderators of the abusive supervision-proactive behavior relationships.

I focus on abusive supervision because it is more often used in destructive supervision literature. Abusive supervisors tend to remind subordinates of past mistakes, humiliate them in front of others, make subordinates have negative feelings, and doubt their capabilities. Besides, it has been shown to increase psychological distress and anxiety (Nandkeolyar, Shaffer, Li, Ekkirala & Bagger, 2014; Tepper, 2000). Following this reasoning, I theorize that abusive supervision is negatively related to individual proactivity.

2.9.2　Potential Moderators

To solve the issue of potential moderators, I examine the factors that affect the strength of the relationship between abusive supervision and proactive behavior. Proactive behavior literature has considered the moderating role of personal factors in influencing the effect of situational antecedents. Given the significance organizational identification has for an individual (Ashforth, Harrison & Corley, 2008), not much is known about its moderating effect on the relation between situational factors and proactive behavior. Therefore, I argue that organizational identification moderates the abusive supervision-proactive behavior association.

In abusive supervision research, the moderating role of organizational identification has been theorized and tested by a few studies. For example, Decoster et al. (2013) conducted a study using a sample of 224 employees and found that organizational identification buffered the negative relationship between abusive supervision and perceived connection with colleagues and the positive relationship between abusive supervision and tendency to gossip about the supervisor. Conversely, Xu et al. (2015) argued that employees with high levels of commitment to organization were more vulnerable under supervisory abuse and hence, responded more negatively. They found support for their argument by using a sample of 456 employees and 78 human resource managers from 78 Chinese organizations. Moreover, Harris et al. (2007) conceptualized identification as meaning of work and found that it intensified the negative impact of abusive supervision on job performance. Similarly, Reilly (1994) found that employees who were highly psychological attached to their organization tent to experience the adverse effects of job stressors more than those who were lowly attached. Clearly, the results were not consistent, suggesting that such moderating effect was contingent. Thus, I propose a model in which employee positive trait affectivity impacts whether organizational identification buffers the negative effect of abusive supervision on proactive behavior.

Transactional model of stress (Lazarus & Folkman, 1984, 1987) is used to explain this model. Drawing from this theory, a person's reaction to a stressor is determined by the interactions between the environment which produces the stressor and the person who appraises it. In addition, the personal variables have many types, such as dispositions, goals and beliefs. Thus, his or her behavioral response is dependent on the interaction of the stressor and the personal factors. Following this logic, I argue that positive trait affectivity, as an important affective disposition of proactive behavior, can influence the moderating effect of organizational identification–believing that one is a member of his or her organization, on the abusive supervision–proactive behavior association. Because "negative environmental cues may serve to bring about heightened levels of sensitivity for those who ordinarily are predisposed to perceive positive stimuli" (Hochwarter et al., 2003, p. 1021), I suggest that high positive trait affectivity exacerbates the negative effect of abusive supervision on proactive behavior of individuals with low organizational identification.

In sum, to address these emerging issues in the proactivity literature, I firstly propose a model in which abusive supervision is negatively related to proactive behavior and there is a three-way interaction of abusive supervision, organizational identification and positive affectivity in impacting proactive behavior in the next chapter (Chapter 3). Hypotheses are also developed following the model. I then conducted two field studies to test these hypotheses (Chapter 4). Finally, I discuss the implications, limitations and future research directions in Chapter 5.

3 THEORETICAL BACKGROUND AND HYPOTHESES DEVELOPMENT

Abusive supervision can be viewed as a type of interpersonal stressor. It depletes the abused subordinate's physical and cognitive resources, which, in turn, will lead to reduced proactive behavior. Organizational identification can motivate an individual to internalize the organization's goal and spend extra efforts into work. Consequently, it may affect how individuals respond to workplace stressors. Positive affectivity, as an individual attribute, is found to be positively related to proactive concepts. Moreover, it may also play a critical role in influencing individuals' reactions to stress. Thus, a stress perspective is proposed to explain the underlying reasoning of abusive supervision effect.

3.1 Transactional Model of Stress

According to Le Pine, Podsakoff and Le Pine (2005), stressors were defined as "the stimuli that evoke the stress process" (p. 764). In the transactional model of stress, Lazarus and Folkman (1987) suggested that a person's response to a stressor was determined by the interplay of person and environment. The environment not only gave rise to the stressor, but included other relevant factors such as support from the source of the stressor or organization (Harris,

Lambert & Harris, 2013; Hobman, Restubog, Bordia & Tang, 2009; Lian, Ferris & Brown, 2012). The personal characteristics incorporated psychological, cultural, and trait-related factors such as conscientiousness and positive affectivity (Mawritz et al., 2014; Hochwarter et al., 2003). These factors interactively impacted an individual's behavioral response.

Drawing from this theory, individuals evaluated the potential threat of a stressor based on a two-stage appraisal process. In the primary appraisal stage, individuals determined if the stressor was beneficial or harmful for their personal growth. Then, in the secondary appraisal stage, individuals determined if he or she needed to do something to eliminate the stressor (problem-directed coping strategy) or to reduce the negative emotional impact of the stressor (emotion-directed coping strategy; Lazarus, 1995; Lazarus & Folkman, 1984, 1987). Although a given stressor may be perceived as more or less harmful from individual to individual, abusive supervision is likely to be a phenomenon that is interpreted homogenously across individuals as a highly salient, negative stressor (Nandkeolyar et al., 2014). Nevertheless, decisions about how to respond to the stressor may differ largely across employees. Therefore, this research focuses on the secondary appraisal stage by exploring the moderating effects of organizational identification and positive affectivity on stress reactions.

Previous research has suggested that individuals engage in problem-directed coping when they believe they can effectively change the stressor; whereas individuals use emotion-directed coping when the threatening stressor is perceived as less controllable (Folkman, Lazarus, Gruen & DeLongis, 1986). Since subordinates often do not have the power to alter abusive supervisors (Mawritz et al., 2014), I focus on one form of subordinates' emotion-directed coping: proactive behavior.

On the basis of transactional model of stress, researchers have argued that a stressor can consume the physical energy and resources of employees, create situations of information overload, and narrow their perceptual attention. Consequently, employees have fewer resources left, and have to ignore possible problems and useful information in their work activities (e.g., Gilboa, Shirom, Fried & Cooper, 2008; Nandkeolyar et al., 2014). Empirically, it was found that stressors were positively related to employees' emotional exhaustion (Aryee et al., 2008), and negatively associated with supervisors' support (Xu, Huang, Lam & Miao, 2012), employees' job performance (Gilboa et al., 2008), organizational citizenship behaviors (Zellars et al., 2002), as well as constructive suggestion-making (Li et al., 2009).

3.2 Abusive Supervision and Proactive Behavior

Tepper (2000) firstly defined abusive supervision as "subordinates' perceptions of the extent to which their supervisors engage in sustained display of hostile verbal and nonverbal behaviors, excluding physical contact" (p. 178). Examples of such supervisory mistreatments include giving others the silent treatment, humiliating someone in front of others, withholding needed information, and making aggressive eye contact (Aryee et al., 2008; Tepper et al., 2011; Xu et al., 2012). This definition shows a few interesting aspects of these supervisory actions. First, abusive supervision is a subjective perception or evaluation which means the abusive levels of supervisors' negative behaviors will differ among subordinates. Second, abusive supervision is not just a one-time event, but a type of sustained and repetitive behaviors. Third, abusive supervisory behaviors contain both hostile verbal and nonverbal behaviors, but exclude physical contact. In the end, abusive supervision refers to the behaviors themselves, but not the intentions of the actions.

Although abusive supervision is not a high base rate phenomenon, it has been found to be linked to organizational deviance, psychological distress, job

3 THEORETICAL BACKGROUND AND HYPOTHESES DEVELOPMENT

and family dissatisfaction, problem drinking, organizational commitment and fear (Aryee et al., 2007; Aryee et al., 2008; Martinko et al., 2013; Tepper, 2007; Tepper et al., 2009). To explore the underlying psychological mechanisms of the aforementioned relationships, researchers have drawn from theoretical perspectives such as transactional model of stress, conservation of resources theory, social exchange theory, social learning theory, reactance theory and the theory of displaced aggression (Aryee et al., 2008; Lian et al., 2012; Liu, Liao & Loi, 2012; Mitchell & Ambrose, 2007; Nandkeolyar et al., 2014; Wang et al., 2012; Xu et al., 2012; Zellars et al., 2002).

A number of moderating factors have been suggested to explain the inconsistent findings in terms of outcomes of abusive supervision (Martinko et al., 2013; Tepper, 2007). Martinko and the coauthors' (2013) review classified them into several categories, including situational factors, supervisor characteristics and behaviors, and subordinate characteristics and behaviors. To be more specific, situational moderators contained not only organization-level factors such as organizational structure and work climates, but also team-level factors such as team member support, and coworkers' approval of workplace deviance. It has been identified that supervisor-level moderators referred to supervisors' hostility, supportive behavior, and leader-member exchange. Last but not the least, subordinate characteristics and behaviors have received the most scholarly attention and contained personality traits, self-esteem, norm of reciprocity, meaning of work, subordinates' attribution for abusive supervision and susceptibility to emotional contagion, and demographic variables. However, there are also some inconsistent findings for the moderators in the abusive supervision-work consequences relationships.

In order to start proactive behavior, an individual needs to possess enough resources and spend additional effort (Frese, Fay, Hilburger, Leng & Tag, 1997). As mentioned above, an abused subordinate will have fewer resources left and be reluctant to spend resources and extra effort to bring about changes, especially when these changes can be controlled by themselves. Moreover, for an individual to engage in proactive behavior, it is necessary for them to anticipate the future and realize the possible or potential problems at work (Grant & Ashford, 2008). Under an abusive supervisor, the individual will worry about the future and be distracted from his or her job. Therefore, abusive supervisors tend to demotivate their subordinates to engage in proactive behaviors.

There has been some evidence from extant literature. A few studies have indicated that under stressful work environments, individuals were likely to cope by reducing their behaviors that were beneficial for the organization and others (e.g., Aryee et al., 2008; Rafferty & Restubog, 2011; Xu et al., 2012). For instance, Aryee and the coauthors (2008) investigated three manufacturing companies in north-eastern China and found that supervisors' abusive actions made their subordinates feel emotionally exhausted, and thus, these subordinates were less likely to take the initiative to solve a work-related problem. The study of Rafferty and Restubog (2011) used a sample of bank employees in the Philippines, and tested the relationship between abusive supervision and prosocial voice. They reported that abusive supervision was significantly and negatively associated with subordinates' frequencies to make recommendations concerning issues that affect the organization. Extending this line of research, I propose that:

Hypothesis 1: Abusive supervision is negatively related to employee proactive behavior.

3.3 The Roles of Organizational Identification and Positive Affectivity

As mentioned above, employee's organizational identification and positive affectivity play a role in the relationship between abusive supervision and employee proactive behavior.

3.3.1 Organizational Identification

Organizational identificationwas rooted in social identity theory (Tajfel & Turner, 1979; Turner, 1982, 1985). This theory proposed that a person's self-concept was based not only on a personal identity (e.g., traits, abilities, and interests), but also on a social identity (e.g., membership in work organizations), and that the former was traditionally regarded as being the obverse of the latter. Specifically, social identity was defined as "that part of an individual's self-concept which derives from his knowledge of his membership of a social group (or groups) together with the value and emotional significance attached to that membership" (Tajfel, 1978, p. 67). Social identity theory assumed that: (a) individuals strived for a positive self-image; (b) parts of an individual's self-concept derived from his or her social identity; and (c) a positive social identity could be protected or enhanced through comparisons with relevant out-group members.

Accordingly, social identification was defined as the perception of oneness with some human aggregate, such as group, team and organization (Ashforth & Mael, 1989). As such, organizational identification reflected an individual's belief of being a member of his or her organization. When individuals strongly identified with their organizations, the organization-based contents of their self-concepts were salient and central (Dutton et al., 1994). Organizational identification aligned one's goals with those of the organization, and promoted motivation, extra-role performance and favorable work behaviors (e.g., Blader & Tyler, 2009; Riketta, 2005; Van Dick & Wagner, 2002). Therefore, organizational identification may have a positive influence on individual proactivity because employees who identify with their organization tend to take the organization's goal as their own, voluntarily learn new knowledge (Walumbwa, Cropanzano &

Hartnell, 2009), discover potential problems at work (Liu et al., 2010) and promote change (Fuchs & Edwards, 2011).

Applying to stress research, the social identity perspective suggested that social identity salience was influential in the stress process because (a) the salience of an individual's social identity impacted whether a stressor was evaluated as self-threatening (i.e., primary appraisal). Consistently, if an individual's social identity was salient, his or her appraisal of stressors would be impacted by his or her in-group views, and (b) social identity salience also played a fundamental role in active coping processes (i.e., secondary appraisal) because it served as a basis for the receipt of social support from other in-group members (Haslam & Reicher, 2006). Because of the target issue, the present research follows the convention (Decoster et al., 2013) and focuses on the moderating role of organizational identification in the secondary appraisal stage.

Pertaining to such moderating role of organizational identification, the majority of researchers have found support for a buffering effect of organizational identification on reactions to a workplace stressor (Haslam, Jetten & Waghorn, 2009; Schaubroeck & Jones, 2000; Yang, Johnson, Zhang, Spector & Xu, 2013). For example, Wegge, Schuh and van Dick (2012) conducted an experiment with 96 call center agents and reported that organizational identification worked as a resource in coping with stressors and buffered their negative effects. Similarly, Decoster et al. (2013) argued that when an organizational identity was salient, employees under stressful conditions were more likely to protect their organization's image and minimize the differences within the organization. Consequently, they gossiped less about their supervisor and perceived higher levels of cohesion. They collected data and found support for these arguments.

Conversely, a few researchers have contended that organizational identification may not be effective and sometimes has a strengthening effect on stress reactions (Frisch, Häusser, van Dick & Mojzisch, 2014). According to previous research, employees highly identified with organizations were more likely

3 THEORETICAL BACKGROUND AND HYPOTHESES DEVELOPMENT

to receive organizational support. Several experimental studies demonstrated that under stressful situations, organizational support might be perceived as a threat to their self-esteem and result in feelings of being ineffective. As a consequence, employees' reactions were more severe (Bolger & Amarel, 2007; Bolger, Zuckerman & Kessler, 2000; Maisel & Gable, 2009). Take Maisel and Gable's (2009) as an example, it has been found that the receipt of actual support from close others is often related to negative outcomes such as sad and anxious emotion.

Furthermore, a paucity of field studies reported that when employees identified with their organization and derived a wide set of meanings, they were more sensitive to negative environments, and finally, they responded more negatively (Harris et al., 2007; Reilly, 1994; Xu et al., 2015). More narrowly, Harris et al. (2007) invited participants from an automotive U.S. company, and found that the detrimental effect of abusive supervision was higher when the subordinates derived more meanings from their activities in the organization. In addition, the study of Reilly (1994) utilized a sample of over 500 hospital nurses. The moderated regression analyses showed that the linkage between workplace stressors and burnout (i.e., emotional exhaustion) was significantly stronger for nurses who were more committed. Finally, Xu et al. (2015) used data from 456 employees and 78 human resource managers in various Chinese companies, and found that under abusive supervision, employees who highly identified with their organizations tent to act more negatively by withholding their concerns and suggestions.

In summary, organizational identification may play a critical role in predicting proactive behavior. But under stressful circumstances, its role is more complex. Hence, it is useful to explore possible boundary conditions of the moderating role of organizational identification.

3.3.2 Positive Affectivity

As previously mentioned, personality factors are another type of moderators thatdeserve investigation in the present study (Hochwarter et al., 2003). Individual difference variables play a crucial role in the stress process because dispositions strongly impact appraisals of stressful situations (Ganster & Schaubroeck, 1991). Therefore, whether abusive supervision is perceived as a threat or an opportunity is dependent not only on an individual's beliefs, but on that individual's dispositions. Furthermore, Bolger and Zuckerman (1995) contended that personality moderated the impacts of stressful events on outcomes. In line with previous research (Harvey et al., 2007), I investigate positive affectivity as a moderator in the association between environmental stressors and consequences.

Positive trait affectivity (PA) reflects one of the two major dimensions of human affective disposition-the other being negative trait affectivity. PA refers to a person's generalized tendency to experience intense pleasant feelings and interpret environmental stimuli in a positive way (Watson & Clark, 1992). People with high PA tend to feel enthusiastic, highly energetic, and jovial. Such individuals experience an overall sense of well-being, have confidence in themselves, and view themselves as actively engaged both interpersonally and in terms of achievement. Additionally, they perceive stimuli, think and act in a manner supportive of positive feelings (Epitropaki & Martin, 2005). Conversely, people with low PA tend to feel of lethargic, apathetic, and sluggish. Such individuals are not supportive of positive feelings through their perceptions, thoughts and behaviors (George, 1992; Watson & Clark, 1984; Watson & Tellegen, 1985).

Affective constructs (i.e., PA) have received considerable attention over the past two decades (Barsade & Gibson, 2007; Kaplan, Bradley, Luchman & Haynes, 2009). Relevantly, positive trait affectivity has been linked to proactive behavior because it provides employees with necessary resources and buffer to cope with any negative feelings in the proactive process. For example, Den Hartog and Belschak (2007) used a sample of 395 employees of a large hospital in The Netherlands and found support for a positive association between trait PA and personal initiative. Likewise, Bindl and Parker (2012) reviewed the previous studies and found general support for a positive effect of high-activated positive affectivity on proactive behavior. Furthermore, Madrid and the coauthors (2014) used a sample of 92 individuals from 73 different companies in Chile and reported that high-activated positive mood (i. e., enthusiastic, inspired) could lead to the creation of new ideas for difficult issues.

Evidence regarding the role of positive affectivity in the stress process is somewhat divergent. On one hand, it is argued that PA can act as resources reducing the negative effects of workplace stressors (Harvey et al., 2007; Zellars, Perrewe, Hochwarter & Anderson, 2006). More specifically, Harvey et al. (2007) conducted a survey including 715 participants from a wide range of occupations such as bricklayer, custodian, director of marketing, loan officer, and vice-president of sales, and reported that individuals with higher positive affectivity were more likely to effectively use ingratiation as a means of establishing support and gaining coping resources that supplement or replace those consumed by abusive supervisory treatments. In addition, Zellars and the coauthors (2006) surveyed 188 nurses in a large hospital in the southeastern United States and found that positive affectivity, working as a reserve to manage threats and enhance resilience, could reduce these nurses' burnout and job tensions.

On the other hand, it is possible that individuals with high PA are more negatively impacted by workplace stressors and dissatisfaction at work (e. g., Duffy et al., 1998; Goussinsky, 2011; Hochwarter et al., 2003; Judge, 1993; Shaw, Duffy, Abdulla & Singh, 2000). It may be that individuals with high PA react much more intensively to work environment, compared to those with low PA (Larsen & Ketelaar, 1991). Specifically, individuals with low PA are prone to be happy in favorable situations but the level of happiness may be lower than that of individuals with high PA. Individuals with low PA are argued to respond to unfavorable events with apathy and listlessness. Conversely, individuals high in PA may be inclined to become tense and sensitive in bad or unfavorable situations and then may undergo an equally intense reaction to negative events as to positive events (Duffy et al., 1998; Hochwarter et al., 2003).

Following the majority of extant research, this study suggests that when organizational identification is low, by being more sensitive to negative environments, and viewing the negative attributes of stressors as a contradiction to their positive affective trait, high-PA individuals will experience exacerbated harmful effects of stressors than their low counterparts.

3.4 The Three-Way Effects of Abusive Supervision, Organizational Identification and Positive Affectivity

The interactional perspective contends that situational factors such as abusive supervision are likely to have a greater or smaller effect when subordinates' personal factors exacerbate or inhibit such external impact (Pervin, 1989; Mitchell & Ambrose, 2007). That is, employees' internal characteristics affect the destructiveness of supervisory mistreatment: supervisory abuse has a weaker effect on employees who perceive themselves as members in their organization than those who do not (Decoster et al., 2013). Consistent with this contention, research on proactive behavior also suggests that supervisors have diverse influence on different subordinates' proactive actions (e.g., Jassen & Gao, 2013), although there has been little research on the impact of abusive supervision on proactive behavior. Proactive behavior is characterized as self-initiated and change-oriented, and involves vocal actions (Parker et al., 2006). Fuller et al. (2006)

3 THEORETICAL BACKGROUND AND HYPOTHESES DEVELOPMENT

argued that organizational identification related to constructive and change - oriented suggestion-making behaviors because they had the desire to see their organization succeed. Hence, it is necessary to take organizational identification into consideration when examining the abusive supervision and proactivity linkage.

Employees with high levels of organizational identification are likely to take their organization's goal as their own and receive a large amount of support from the organization (Ashforth & Mael, 2008; Haslam & Reicher, 2006). This likelihood, under the condition of supervisory abuse, may be particularly useful because it provides employees with resources and enables them to cope with the negative environmental stimuli. Paradoxically, there has been inconsistent evidence regarding the moderating role of organizational identification in the relationship between workplace stressor and employee behavior. The reason may be that such moderating effect is also dependent on individual affective disposition (Hochwarter et al., 2003).

More specifically, employees with low levels of organizational identification will suffer more from abusive supervisory behaviors (such as humiliation in front of others, public criticism and silence treatment) if they are high in positive affectivity, because both the supervisor and organization provide negative information and high PA subordinates tend to be more sensitive. Furthermore, given the nature of the proactive process, employees may experience resource loss and uncertainty, and may need help and guidance from significant others in the workplace, especially the organization and their leaders. If they are high in positive affectivity, they should react more intensively to the mismatches between their affective disposition and work environment. Therefore, they will feel very incapable of being proactive. This line of argument is in agreement with the premise in the positive affectivity literature that individual positive affectivity exacerbates the harmful effects of workplace stressors (Hochwarter et al., 2003).

In contrast, if employees highly identify with their organization, they may not take their supervisors' unfavorable treatments so seriously, and hence do not react so negatively and withhold a lot of self-initiated actions. This buffering effect is not likely to be altered by the degree of positive affectivity, as the environment sends out mixed information. For individuals with high positive affectivity, they are happy, and possess valuable resources (Fredrickson, 1998) to cope with the effect of supervisory abuse. For individuals with low positive affectivity, although generally apathetic, they are likely to utilize the resources provided by their in-groups and overcome the detrimental impact of supervisory abuse. This theory is consistent with the proposition that organizational identification buffers the negative impacts of workplace stressors (Decoster et al., 2013). Consequently, abusive supervision, when combined with low levels of organizational identification and high levels of positive affectivity can enable subordinates to respond most negatively by performing fewest proactive actions.

In sum, I propose that when organizational identification is low, abused subordinates should engage in fewer proactive behaviors when positive affectivity is high (rather than low). On the other hand, when organizational identification is high, positive affectivity may lose its moderating role in the abusive supervision—proactive behavior association. Essentially, I suggest that there is a three-way interaction of abusive supervision, organizational identification and positive affectivity on impacting proactive behavior. Thus, I hypothesize:

Hypothesis 2: Abusive supervision, organizational identification and positive affectivity interact to impact subordinate proactive behavior in such a way that when organizational identification is low and positive affectivity is high, the relationship between abusive supervision and proactive behavior is the most negative.

METHODOLOGY AND RESEARCH DESIGN

4.1 Overview of the Two Studies

The aims of the present research were to test the impact of abusive supervision and the interactive impact of abusive supervision, organizational identification and positive affectivity on subordinate proactivity. To accomplish these, I collected data from two samples of employees from different industries and professional backgrounds, and this increased the generalizability of my findings. In Study 1, multisource survey data were collected to examine the three-way interaction of abusive supervision, organizational identification, and positive affectivity on personal initiative. I measured employee perceived abusive supervision, employee organizational identification, employee positive affectivity and supervisor perceived employee personal initiative. In Study 2, I also collected multisource survey data and used measures of organizational, supervisory and coworker-directed proactive behaviors to test the generalizability of the findings in Study 1 beyond personal initiative.

4.2　Study 1

In this section, a multisource field study was conducted to test the hypotheses. Four key measures were adopted: abusive supervision, organizational identification, positive affectivity and personal initiative. Personal initiative is one of the earliest concepts developed by proactivity researchers (Grant & Ashford, 2008). It describes the fundamental features of individual proactivity. Therefore, it has been widely used as an appropriate measure in empirical studies (i.e., Fritz, Yankelevich, Zarubin & Barger, 2010; Ohly & Fritz, 2007; Salanova & Schaufeli, 2008; Sonnentag, 2003). Following the convention, I used personal initiative as an indicator of proactive behavior in this study. Thus, the hypotheses are now reframed as follows:

Hypothesis 1a: Abusive supervision is negatively related to employee personal initiative.

Hypothesis 2a: Abusive supervision, organizational identification and positive affectivity interact to impact subordinate personal initiative in such a way that when organizational identification is low and positive affectivity is high, the relationship between abusive supervision and personal initiative is the most negative.

4.2.1　Sample and Procedure

Dentists and their immediate supervisors from two hospitals in China agreed to participate in this research. Survey questionnaires were collected in two waves.

4 METHODOLOGY AND RESEARCH DESIGN

The first survey package was only distributed to dentists. It included a cover letter, a questionnaire and a pre-stamped envelope. The cover letter guaranteed confidentiality of responses to avoid problems pertaining to social desirability bias, and explained the aim of the survey and the following survey after three weeks. The questionnaire included abusive supervision and demographic variables. About three weeks later, separate survey packages were administered to dentists and their direct supervisors. The dentists responded to survey questions on organizational identification and positive affectivity. Their direct supervisors evaluated their personal initiative. All completed questionnaires were mailed directly to the researcher using the pre-stamped envelope contained in the package.

To match dentists' two responses and those of their supervisors, these dentists were required to write down the first characters of their given name and family name; supervisors, for their part, were asked to indicate the name of each rated subordinate. In addition, to ensure data quality, problematic cases were screened out according to the following criteria: (1) questionnaires without the dentists' name; (2) questionnaires with the same answers to all measurement items; (3) questionnaires where supervisors evaluated all their subordinates in the same manner; and (4) questionnaires without all three responses. As a result, 165 valid questionnaire sets were collected, constituting a valid response rate of 90.2 percent. Of the 165 subordinates, 45.5 percent were men and 54.5 percent were women. 30.3 percent were 26 to 30 years old; 30.3 percent were 31 to 35 years old; 18.8 percent were 36 to 40 years old and 12.1 percent were more than 41 years old. The average organizational tenure was 98.64 months. 16.4 percent had a vocational degree or lower, 32.1 percent had a bachelor degree and 51.5 percent had a master or higher degree. 12.1 percent of the employees had worked with their supervisor for less than one year, 23.0 percent had worked with their supervisor for 1 to 3 years, and 64.8 percent had worked with their supervisor for more than 3 years. Of the supervisors, 77 percent were male, and 23 percent were female.

4.2.2 Measures

All measures used in the present study were originally developed in English. Since data were collected in China, I followed the conventional translation and back-translation procedures (Brislin, 1980) to translate all English items into Chinese. First, items were translated into the Chinese language by the researcher and another Ph. D. student separately. And then they were translated back into English by other two Ph. D. students. All of the three Ph. D. students were native Chinese speakers but fluent in English. If there were disagreements between the two English scales, we would discuss together and reach agreements on how to revise the questionable items appropriately. The measures used in this study were briefly presented in the following sections.

Abusive supervision. Abusive supervision was measured by using the 5-item short-version of Tepper (2000), which has also been used in other studies (Mitchell & Aambrose, 2007). A sample item included: "My supervisor lies to me." All items were completed on a 5-point scale ranging from 1 (strongly disagree) to 5 (strongly agree).

Organizational identification. Organizational identification was measured by using Mael and Ashforth's (1992) 6-item scale. A sample item was: "This hospital's successes are my successes." All items were completed on a 7-point scale ranging from 1 (strongly disagree) to 7 (strongly agree).

Positive affectivity. Positive affectivity was measured with 5 items from the short-form of the Positive and Negative Affective Schedule (Thompson, 2007). The subordinates indicated how they generally felt in terms of 5 positive adjectives (e. g., active, inspired). All items were completed on a 5-point scale ranging from 1 (not at all) to 5 (extremely).

Personal initiative. Personal initiative was assessed by using Frese and coworkers' (1997) 7-item personal initiative scale. A sample item was: "This employee takes initiative immediately even when others don't." All items were completed on a 5-point scale ranging from 1 (strongly disagree) to 5 (strongly agree).

Control variables. Previous studies have consistently found that age, gender, education, tenure with organization and tenure with supervisor can influence employee proactive behaviors (e.g., Le Pine & Van Dyne, 1998; Fay & Frese, 2001). Thus, I included these variables as control variables. More specifically, age was measured in years, and gender was dummy coded as 0=male and 1=female. Education was divided into three levels: (1) "Lower vocational degree or less"; (2) "bachelor degree"; and (3) "master degree or more". Tenure with organization was measured with one item asking for the number of months in the organization. Tenure with the supervisor was coded as 1=less than a year, 2=1 to 3 years, 3=more than 3 years.

4.2.3 Analytical Approach

Data analysis consisted of factor analysis, reliability analysis, correlation analysis and a series of moderated regression analyses by applying HLM 6.0, SPSS 22.0, and LISREL 8.80. First, a confirmatory factor analysis (CFA) was conducted to ensure discriminant validity of two variables, organizational identification and positive affectivity. Multiple indices of fit were calculated to evaluate the models (Kelloway, 1996). A large chi-square value meant that the model did not fit the data well. I reported the comparative fit index (CFI; Bentler, 1990) and the nonnormed fit index (NNFI; Hoyle, 1995), for which values more than 0.90 are desired, the root mean square error of approximation (RMSEA; Browne & Cudeck, 1993), for which values less than 0.08 are acceptable. Second, descriptive statistics and correlation matrix were shown.

Then, given that each supervisor provided ratings for more than one subordinate, HLM version 6.0 (Raudenbush & Bryk, 2002) was used to test the hypotheses. In this study, abusive supervision, organizational identification, positive affectivity, and controls were at the individual-level (level 1). There were no variables at the group-level (level 2) in the analysis. Following Hofmann and Gavin (1998), all the predictor variables were grand-mean-centered in the models, that is, every case of that variable subtracted the overall mean of each of the predictors.

To test Hypothesis 1a, I examined a model where abusive supervision at Level 1 was modeled to have a main effect on personal initiative (with the addition of organizational identification, positive affectivity and control variables) at Level 1. To test Hypothesis 2a, I examined a model where positive affectivity was modeled to interact with abusive supervision-organizational identification interaction in predicting personal initiative.

4.2.4 Results

Confirmatory factor analyses (CFA) were conducted to examine discriminant validity of organizational identification and positive affectivity (James, Mulaik & Brett, 1982). A two-factor model demonstrated good fit to the data (χ^2 = 24.88, df = 13, CFI = 0.98, NNFI = 0.97, RMSEA = 0.08). This model provided a more satisfactory fit than a one-factor model in which the two variables were combined (χ^2 = 73.12, df = 14, CFI = 0.92, NNFI = 0.88, RMSEA = 0.16). Moreover, a chi-square difference test indicated that the two-factor model was significantly better than the alternative one-factor model ($\Delta\chi^2$ = 48.24, Δdf = 1, p<0.01). Therefore, it was reasonable to treat the two variables as distinct constructs.

Next, given the nonindependence of supervisory ratings of personal initiative, I conducted a one-way analysis of variance (ANOVA) with personal initiative as the dependent variable. The results showed that supervisors differed significantly in how they reported their employees on personal initiative (F [40, 124] =

2.517, p<0.01; ICC [1] =0.27). Therefore, it was both appropriate and necessary to model supervisory ratings of personal initiative as being nonindependent.

Table 4.1 summarizes the descriptive statistics and correlation matrix of abusive supervision, organizational identification, positive affectivity, personal initiative and control variables. As shown in Table 4.1, abusive supervision is significantly and negatively related to personal initiative ($r = -0.16$, $p<0.05$). This provides preliminary support to Hypothesis 1a.

I first entered the subordinates' sex, age, education, tenure with organization, and tenure with supervisor at Level 1 as controls in all the models for testing Hypotheses 1a and 2a (see Table 4.2). Since most of the control variables did not have significant coefficients with the dependent variable, I reported the coefficients regarding these demographic variables in Appendix C. In Model 1, abusive supervision was negatively related to personal initiative (see Model 1, $\gamma = -0.14$, $p<0.01$). Hypothesis 1a was supported. Hypothesis 2a predicted a three-way interaction of abusive supervision, organizational identification and positive affectivity in predicting personal initiative. Thus, in Model 2, all of the two-way interactive terms were first entered. In Model 3, consistent with this prediction, the three-way interaction term was positively related to personal initiative (see Model 3, $\gamma = 0.10$, $p<0.05$) (see Figure 4.1). Further simple slope tests indicated that, when organizational identification was low (-1 s.d.), the relationship between abusive supervision and personal initiative was more significantly negative for subordinates with high positive affectivity ($+1$ s.d., simple slope $= -0.53$, $p<0.01$) than for those with low positive affectivity (-1 s.d.; simple slope $= -0.19$, $p<0.05$). This was consistent with my prediction. On the other hand, when organizational identification was high ($+1$ s.d.), the relationship between abusive supervision and personal initiative became insignificant both for subordinates with high positive affectivity ($+1$ s.d., simple slope $= 0.04$, n.s.) and for those with low positive affectivity (-1 s.d.; simple slope $= -0.02$, n.s.). Consequently, Hypothesis 2a was supported.

TABLE 4.1 Descriptive Statistics for Study 1

Variable	M	SD	1	2	3	4	5	6	7	8
1. Abusive supervision	1.80	0.64	(0.84)							
2. Positive affectivity	3.41	0.49	-0.11	(0.60)						
3. Organizational identification	5.09	1.08	-0.20**	0.44**	(0.85)					
4. Personal initiative	3.18	0.72	-0.16*	0.17*	0.18*	(0.92)				
5. Age	33.61	6.90	0.14	0.08	-0.08	0.12	—			
6. Gender	0.55	0.50	-0.10	0.09	0.11	-0.05	0.01	—		
7. Education	2.35	0.75	0.06	-0.00	0.07	0.26**	0.01	-0.17*	—	
8. Tenure with organization	98.64	85.44	0.10	0.07	-0.08	0.04	0.86**	0.09	-0.24**	—
9. Tenure with supervisor	2.53	0.70	0.21*	0.02	-0.08	0.02	0.40**	-0.01	-0.01	0.41**

Notes: N = 165. Coefficient alphas are shown on the diagonal in parentheses.

* p<0.05. ** p<0.01.

TABLE 4.2 Regressions for Abusive Supervision, Positive Affectivity, Organizational Identification and Personal Initiative in Study 1

Model	Personal initiative		
	b	s.e.	t
Model 1			
Abusive supervision	**−0.14****	0.04	−3.13
Positive affectivity	0.10*	0.04	2.50
Organizational identification	0.14*	0.06	2.25
R^2	0.15		
Model 2			
Abusive supervision (AS)	−0.13**	0.04	−3.04
Positive affectivity (PA)	0.10*	0.04	2.38
Organizational identification (OI)	0.10*	0.05	2.08
AS×PA	−0.09	0.05	−1.91
AS×OI	0.18*	0.09	2.14
PA×OI	−0.01	0.05	−0.14
R^2	0.16		
Model 3			
Abusive supervision (AS)	−0.17**	0.05	−3.55
Positive affectivity (PA)	0.12**	0.04	2.76
Organizational identification (OI)	0.10	0.05	2.16
AS×PA	−0.07	0.05	−1.58
AS×OI	0.19*	0.08	2.18
PA×OI	−0.01	0.05	−0.19
AS×PA×OI	0.10*	0.04	2.74
R^2	0.19		

Notes: N = 165. The R^2 values are computed by using SPSS. Control values are not reported in this table.
* $p < 0.05$, ** $p < 0.01$.

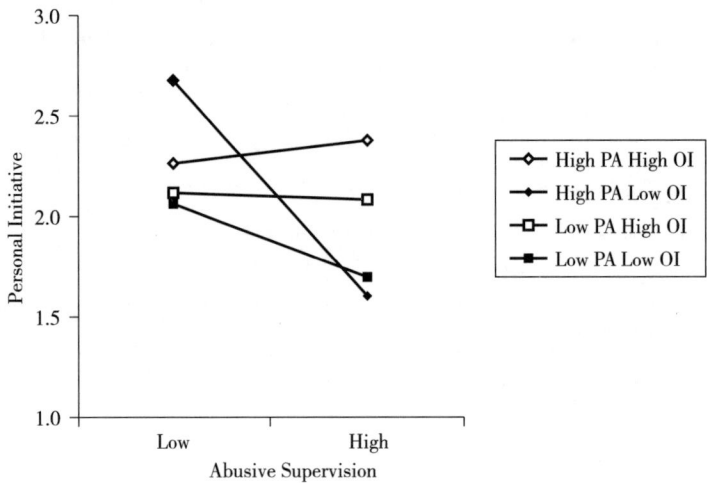

FIGURE 4.1 Plot of the Three-Way Interaction on Personal Initiative in Study 1

4.2.5 Discussion

The mainpurposes of this study were twofold: first, to examine the effect of abusive supervision on subordinate proactive behavior; and second, to evaluate the interactive effect of abusive supervision, organizational identification and positive affectivity on subordinate proactive behavior. Data from 165 dentist – supervisor dyads were collected to test these two hypotheses. Results indicated that the influence of abusive supervision on proactive behavior was significantly negative and the three – way interaction of abusive supervision, organizational identification and positive affectivity on proactive behavior was also significant. Further analyses showed that positive affectivity intensified the negative effect of abusive supervision on proactive behavior of employees who were low in organizational identification.

Although this study has strengths, it has some notable limitations. First, this study used personal initiative as an indicator of proactive behavior. However, it is well recognized that personal initiative is unilateral. For example, personal initiative only includes pro-company actions (Grant & Ashford, 2008; Frese & Fay, 2001), and is general and not target-specific (Hornung et al., 2008). Proactivity researchers have called for more studies simultaneously testing several proactive behaviors in terms of targets or types (Grant & Ashord, 2008; Parker & Collins, 2010; Tornau & Frese, 2012). Following the convention in the abusive supervision literature, subordinates' reactions can be directed at supervisor, coworker and organization (Mitchell & Ambrose, 2007; Wang, Mao, Wu & Liu, 2012). Therefore, the effects of abusive supervision on proactive behaviors directed at organizations, supervisors and coworkers need to be further confirmed.

Second, the sample used in Study 1 is dentists, who are considered as knowledge workers. Because knowledge has been found to affect proactive behavior (Fay & Frese, 2001; Kanfer et al., 2001; Ohly et al., 2006), the findings in Study 1 may not be easily generalized to other samples.

To rule out these limitations, in Study 2, I focused on organizational, supervisory and coworker-directed proactive behaviors as the dependent variables and collected data from a sample of employees in a transportation company, most of whom are not highly-educated. The methodology and results of Study 2 are discussed in the following sections.

4.3 Study 2

A multisource field study was conducted to (1) test the negative relationship between abusive supervision and proactive behavior and (2) examine the three-way interactive effect of abusive supervision, organizational identification, and positive affectivity on proactive behavior. Thus, six key variables were measured: abusive supervision, organizational identification, positive affectivity, organizational proactive behavior, supervisory proactive behavior and interpersonal proactive behavior.

Proactive behavior is a self-initiated and change-oriented behavior that is intended to impact the organization, others or self (Belschak & Den Hartog, 2010; Grant & Ashford, 2008; Griffin et al., 2007). Proactivity researchers have mainly emphasized organizations and coworkers as the two important targets of proactive behavior beneficial for an organization. Organizational proactive behavior refers to initiative behaviors directed at the organization (e. g., suggesting ideas for solutions for company problems, optimizing the organization of work to further organizational goals). Coworker-directed proactive behavior refers to initiative behaviors directed at coworkers (e. g., sharing knowledge with coworkers, helping orient new coworkers). The voice literature has suggested that supervisors are the common targets of making suggestions (Liu et al., 2010, 2013). Meanwhile, the stress literature has pointed out that employees are likely to have responses towards supervisors as well as coworkers under a workplace stressor (Wang et al., 2012). Therefore, I refer to supervisory proactive behavior as initiative behaviors directed at the supervisor (e. g., giving constructive suggestions to the supervisor to improve his or her work, communicating opinions about work issues to the supervisor).

Abusive supervision may impact all of three forms of proactive behaviors. From the stress perspective, abusive supervision can be conceptualized as a workplace stressor (Aryee et al., 2008). In addition, it has been theorized that under stressful conditions, employees are required to focus physical energy and resources on dealing with this stressor, tend to experience information overload and have fewer cognitive resources left to anticipate the future and prevent possible problems (Gilboa et al., 2008; Nandkeolyar et al., 2014). According to Mitchell and Ambrose (2007), employees may respond to abusive supervision by engaging in more unfavorable behaviors targeting the organization, supervisor and other individuals. In this study, I argue that abusive supervision may lead to

4 METHODOLOGY AND RESEARCH DESIGN

fewer proactive behaviors towards the organization, supervisors and coworkers. Therefore, I proposed:

Hypothesis 1b: *Abusive supervision is negatively related to employee organizational proactive behavior.*

Hypothesis 1c: *Abusive supervision is negatively related to employee supervisory proactive behavior.*

Hypothesis 1d: *Abusive supervision is negatively related to employee coworker-directed proactive behavior.*

Furthermore, I reframed Hypothesis 2 as follows:

Hypothesis 2b: *Abusive supervision, organizational identification and positive affectivity interact to impact subordinate organizational proactive behavior in such a way that when organizational identification is low and positive affectivity is high, the relationship between abusive supervision and organizational proactive behavior is the most negative.*

Hypothesis 2c: *Abusive supervision, organizational identification and positive affectivity interact to impact subordinate supervisory proactive behavior in such a way that when organizational identification is low and positive affectivity is high, the relationship between abusive supervision and supervisory proactive behavior is the most negative.*

Hypothesis 2d: *Abusive supervision, organizational identification and positive affectivity interact to impact subordinate coworker-directed proactive behavior in such a way that when organizational identification is low and positive affectivity is high, the relationship between abusive supervision and coworker-directed proactive behavior is the most negative.*

4.3.1 Sample and Procedure

Employees and their direct supervisors from a large transportation company in Southeast China were invited to participate in this study. Before distributing questionnaires, I got the approval from senior managers. Survey questionnaires were collected in one wave, but from different sources. Questionnaires from employees and their supervisors were matched by a code decided by the researcher (each supervisor was required to rate only one subordinate). Employees reported their perceived abusive supervision, organizational identification, positive affectivity and demographic information. Supervisors rated their subordinates' organizational, supervisory and coworker-directed proactive behaviors. Respondents returned their completed surveys directly to the researcher and thus confidentiality of their data was assured to avoid problems related to social desirability bias.

I ultimately got feedback from 243 employees and 242 supervisors. After matching the responses from employees and supervisors, I obtained 226 employee-supervisor dyads, with valid response rates of 93.0% and 93.4%, respectively. Of the 226 subordinates, 44.2% of them were male and 55.3% were female. 59.3% were 21 to 25 years old, 30.5% were 26 to 30 years old, 7.5% were 31 to 35 years old and 1.6% was more than 36 years old. The average organizational tenure was 37.48 months. 58.8% had a vocational degree or lower and 40.7% had a bachelor degree. 80.1% of the employees had worked with their supervisor for less than one year, 16.4% had worked with their supervisor for 1 to 3 years, and 3.1% had worked with their supervisor for more than 3 years. Of the supervisors, 38.5% were male, and 61.5% were female.

4.3.2 Measures

Following the same procedure used in Study 1, the measures in the present study were translated into Chinese. With the exceptions of abusive supervision and proactive behaviors, I used the scales mentioned in Study 1 to measure organizational identification, positive affectivity and control variables. They were briefly presented in the following sections. All ratings were completed on a 7-point Likert scale ranging from 1 (*strongly disagree*) to 7 (*strongly agree*).

Organizational proactive behavior. Organizational proactive behavior was measured by using the three-item pro-organizational proactive behavior scale from Belschak and Den Hartog (2010). A sample item is "This employee personally takes the initiative to suggest ideas for solutions for company problems".

Supervisory proactive behavior. Supervisory proactive behavior was measured by using 4 items adapted from Liu et al.'s (2010) speaking up to supervisor scale. A sample item is "This employee communicates his or her opinions about work issues to me even if his or her opinion is different, and I disagree with him or her".

Coworker-directed proactive behavior. Coworker-directed proactive behavior was measured by using the four-item pro-social proactive behavior scale from Belschak and Den Hartog (2010). A sample item is, "This employee personally takes the initiative to share knowledge with colleagues."

Abusive supervision. Abusive supervision was measured by using the 15-item scale of Tepper (2000). This scale has been widely used and has already been tested in Chinese context (e.g., Aryee et al., 2007, 2008). Consistent with previous studies (e.g., Zellars, Tepper & Duffy, 2002), I treated abusive supervision at the individual level. Sample items are "My immediate supervisor ridicules me", and "My immediate supervisor tells me my thoughts or feelings are stupid".

4.3.3 Analytical Approach

Data analysis consisted of factor analysis, reliability analysis, correlation analysis, and a series of moderated regression analyses by applying SPSS 22.0 and

LISREL 8.80. First, a CFA was conducted to ensure discriminant validity of the three forms of proactive behaviors. Next, another CFA was performed on the three self-report constructs, including abusive supervision, organizational identification and positive affectivity, to test construct distinctiveness. Chi-square values and fit indices were used to evaluate these models. Third, descriptive statistics, internal reliabilities and intercorrelations were presented.

Then moderated regression analyses using SPSS 22.0 were employed to test the hypotheses. The predictor variables used in the interaction term were centered to reduce non-essential multicollinearity (Aiken & West, 1991). Subordinates' five demographic variables were also controlled in all the analyses. To test Hypotheses 1b, 1c, and 1d, I regressed abusive supervision, together with organizational identification and positive affectivity, onto organizational, supervisory and coworker-directed proactive behaviors. To test Hypotheses 2b, 2c, and 2d, I examined models where abusive supervision, organizational identification and positive affectivity interactively predicted three foci of proactive behaviors.

4.3.4 Results

Before testing the hypotheses, I conducted a confirmatory factor analysis to test whether the three forms of proactive behaviors were distinct. I compared the three-factor model with three alternative models. The first alternative model was a two-factor model that integrated organizational proactive behavior with supervisory proactive behavior. This two-factor model corresponded to the assumption that supervisory proactive behavior was similar to organizational proactive behavior because supervisors were viewed as representatives of their organizations. The second alternative model was another two-factor model that integrated supervisory proactive behavior with coworker-directed proactive behavior. Such a two-factor model corresponded to the fundamental classification, that is, interpersonal proactive behavior. Finally, the third alternative model was a one-factor model that combined all three forms of proactive behaviors into a single factor.

Table 4.3 shows the results of the four measurement models. The three-factor model provided a satisfactory fit to the data ($X^2 = 76.92$, df = 41, CFI = 0.99, NNFI=0.98, RMSEA=0.06). This model had better fit to the data than the first two-factor model ($\Delta X^2 = 29.16$, $\Delta df = 2$, p<0.01), the other two-factor model ($\Delta X^2 = 78.99$, $\Delta df = 2$, p<0.01), and the one-factor model ($\Delta X^2 = 116.48$, $\Delta df = 3$, p<0.01). Therefore, it was reasonable to view the three variables as distinct.

TABLE 4.3 CFA Results for Three Proactive Behaviors in Study 2

Model	X^2	ΔX^2	df	RMSEA	NNFI	CFI
Three-factor model (OPB, SPB, CPB)	76.92	—	41	0.06	0.98	0.99
Two-factor model (OPB+SPB, CPB)	106.08	29.16**	43	0.08	0.97	0.98
Two-factor model (OPB, SPB+CPB)	155.91	78.99**	43	0.11	0.95	0.96
One-factor model (OPB+SPB+CPB)	193.40	116.48**	44	0.12	0.94	0.95

Notes: N = 226. OPB = Organizational Proactive Behavior, SPB = Supervisory Proactive Behavior, CPB = Coworker-directed Proactive Behavior.

** p<0.01.

Another CFA analysis was conducted to test the discriminant validities of abusive supervision, organizational identification and positive affectivity. I compared the three-factor model with two alternative models. The first alternative model was a two-factor model that integrated organizational identification with positive affectivity. The second alternative model was a one-factor model that combined abusive supervision, organizational identification and positive affectivity into a single factor.

Table 4.4 presents the results of the three measurement models. The three-factor solution provided a better fit to the data ($X^2 = 627.61$, df = 296, CFI = 0.95, NNFI=0.95, RMSEA = 0.07). This solution was more satisfactory than the two-factor model ($\Delta \chi^2$ = 410.95, Δdf = 2, p<0.01), and the one-factor model ($\Delta \chi^2$ = 1810.28, Δdf = 3, p<0.01). Consequently, it was reasonable to treat abusive supervision, organizational identification and positive affectivity as distinctive variables.

TABLE 4.4 CFA Results for Abusive Supervision, Organizational Identification and Positive Affectivity in Study 2

Model	χ^2	$\Delta \chi^2$	Df	RMSEA	NNFI	CFI
Three-factor model (AS, OI, PA)	627.61	—	296	0.07	0.95	0.95
Two-factor model (AS, OI+PA)	1038.56	410.95**	298	0.11	0.91	0.91
One-factor model (AS+OI+PA)	2437.89	1810.28**	299	0.18	0.81	0.82

Notes: N=226. AS=Abusive Supervision, OI=Organizational Identification, PA=Positive Affectivity.
** p<0.01.

Table 4.5 presented the descriptive statistics and correlation matrix for all the variables in the present study. As shown in Table 4.5, abusive supervision was insignificantly related to organizational proactive behavior (r = -0.12, n.s.), but it was significantly and negatively related to supervisory proactive behavior (r = -0.21, p <0.01) and coworker-directed proactive behavior (r = -0.18, p<0.01). As a result, Hypothesis 1b was not supported.

Subordinates' age, gender, education, tenure with organization and tenure with supervisor were also controlled in the following regression analyses, but only a few had significant effects on dependent variables. To highlight the results for key hypotheses, they were only shown in Appendix C. As shown in Table 4.6, for organizational proactive behavior, in Step 1, abusive supervision was not significantly related to organizational proactive behavior (β = -0.07, n.s.). Hypothesis 1b was not supported. Following the conventions of Blickle, Meurs, Wihler, Ewen, Plies and Günther (2013) and Weigl, Müller, Hornung, Zacher and Angerer (2013), I continued to test the interactional hypotheses. In Step 2, all of the two-way interactive effects were entered. Finally, in Step 3, the three-way interaction was significantly and positively related to organizational proactive behavior ($\beta = 0.28$, $p<0.05$) (see Figure 4.2). Further simple slope tests demonstrated that, under the condition of low organizational identification (-1 s. d.), the relationship between abusive supervision and organizational proactive behavior was more significantly negative for subordinates with high positive affectivity ($+1$ s. d., $\beta = -0.45$, $p<0.05$) than for those with low positive affectivity (-1 s. d., $\beta = -0.08$, n. s.). On the other hand, under the condition of high organizational identification ($+1$ s. d.), the effect of abusive supervision become insignificant both for subordinates with high positive affectivity ($+1$ s. d., $\beta = 0.17$, n. s.) than for those with low positive affectivity (-1 s. d., $\beta = -0.17$, n. s.). Consequently, Hypothesis 2b was supported.

For supervisory proactive behavior, in Step 1, abusive supervision was significantly related to supervisory proactive behavior ($\beta = -0.18$, $p<0.05$). Hypothesis 1c was supported. In Step 2, three two-way interactive effects were entered. Finally, in Step 3, the three-way interaction was significantly and positively related to supervisory proactive behavior ($\beta = 0.31$, $p <0.01$) (see Figure 4.3). Further simple slope tests indicated that, when organizational identification was low (-1 s. d.), the relationship between abusive supervision and supervisory proactive behavior was more significantly negative for subordinates with high positive affectivity ($+1$ s. d., $\beta = -0.51$, $p<0.01$) than for those with low positive affectivity (-1 s. d., $\beta = -0.16$, n. s.). This finding was consistent with my prediction. Moreover, when organizational identification was high ($+1$ s. d.), the relationship between abusive supervision and supervisory proactive behavior was significant and negative for subordinates with low positive affectivity (-1 s. d., $\beta = -0.49$, $p<0.05$) but became insignificant for those with high positive affectivity ($+1$ s. d., $\beta = 0.05$, n. s.). Although under the condition of high organizational identification and low positive affectivity, the finding was not exactly in accord with my prediction, generally speaking, Hypothesis 2c was supported.

TABLE 4.5 Descriptive Statistics for Study 2

Variable	M	SD	1	2	3	4	5	6	7	8	9	10
1. Abusive supervision	1.45	0.50	(0.87)									
2. Positive affectivity	5.37	1.01	-0.34**	(0.85)								
3. Organizational identification	5.50	1.08	-0.30**	0.50**	(0.85)							
4. Organizational proactive behavior	5.99	0.78	-0.12	0.16*	0.14*	(0.75)						
5. Supervisory proactive behavior	5.97	0.86	-0.21**	0.13*	0.12	0.68**	(0.84)					
6. Coworker-directed proactive behavior	6.17	0.77	-0.18**	0.17*	0.17**	0.58**	0.70**	(0.84)				
7. Age	25.78	3.70	0.60	-0.02	-0.10	-0.01	-0.00	-0.02	—			
8. Gender	0.56	0.50	-0.11	-0.00	0.10	0.01	0.06	0.07	0.13	—		
9. Education	1.41	0.49	0.02	-0.06	-0.16*	0.03	-0.01	-0.02	0.47**	0.07	—	
10. Tenure with organization	37.48	29.51	0.06	-0.01	-0.04	-0.01	0.02	-0.07	0.70**	0.03	0.48**	—
11. Tenure with supervisor	1.23	0.49	0.05	0.06	0.02	0.04	0.03	0.00	0.17*	-0.08	0.13*	0.26**

Notes: N = 226. Coefficient alphas are shown on the diagonal in parentheses.

* $p<0.05$, ** $p<0.01$.

4 METHODOLOGY AND RESEARCH DESIGN

For coworker-directed proactive behavior, in Step 1, abusive supervision was not significantly related to coworker-directed proactive behavior ($\beta=-0.12$, n.s.). Hypothesis 1d was not supported. In Step 2, three two-way interactive effects were also entered. Finally, in Step 3, the three-way interaction was significantly and positively related to coworker-directed proactive behavior ($\beta = 0.35$, $p<0.01$) (see Figure 4.4). Further simple slope tests demonstrated that, under the condition of low organizational identification (-1 s.d.), the effect of abusive supervision on coworker-directed proactive behavior was more significantly negative for subordinates with high positive affectivity ($+1$ s.d., $\beta = -0.51$, $p<0.01$) than for those with low positive affectivity (-1 s.d., $\beta = -0.07$, n.s.). On the other hand, under the condition of high organizational identification ($+1$ s.d.), the effect of abusive supervision was significant and negative for subordinates with low positive affectivity (-1 s.d., $\beta = -0.36$, $p<0.01$) and was insignificant for those with high positive affectivity ($+1$ s.d., $\beta = 0.08$, n.s.). Therefore, Hypothesis 2d was supported.

TABLE 4.6 Regressions for Abusive Supervision, Positive Affectivity, Organizational Identification and Proactive Behaviors in Study 2

Step 2	OPB	SPB	CPB
Step 1			
Abusive supervision	−0.07	−0.18*	−0.12
Positive affectivity	0.10	0.06	0.08
Organizational identification	0.08	0.04	0.10
R^2 (F-change)	0.04 (2.71*)	0.06 (3.83*)	0.06 (3.97**)
Step 2			
Abusive supervision (AS)	−0.09	−0.22**	−0.17*
Positive affectivity (PA)	0.08	0.05	0.08
Organizational identification (OI)	0.10	0.04	0.10
AS×PA	−0.10	−0.05	−0.12

续表

Step 2	OPB	SPB	CPB
AS×OI	0.09	−0.01	0.01
PA×OI	0.06	0.08	−0.03
R^2 (F-change)	0.05 (0.74)	0.07 (0.74)	0.07 (0.68)
Step 3			
Abusive supervision (AS)	−0.16	−0.31**	−0.27**
Positive affectivity (PA)	0.14	0.12	0.15
Organizational identification (OI)	0.16	0.10	0.17*
AS×PA	−0.01	0.06	0.00
AS×OI	0.16	0.06	0.09
PA×OI	0.13	0.15	0.06
AS×PA×OI	0.28*	0.31**	0.35**
R^2 (F-change)	0.08 (6.38*)	0.10 (8.37**)	0.12 (10.73**)

Notes: N = 226. Standardized regression coefficients are presented. Control variables are not reported.
* $p < 0.05$, ** $p < 0.01$.

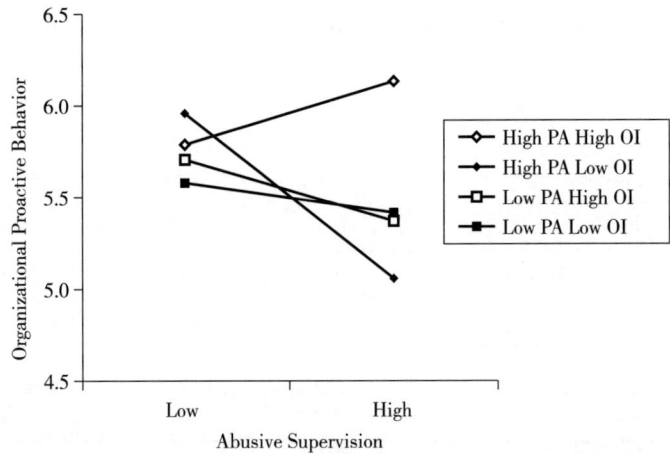

FIGURE 4.2 Plot of the Three-Way Interaction on Organizational Proactive Behavior in Study 2

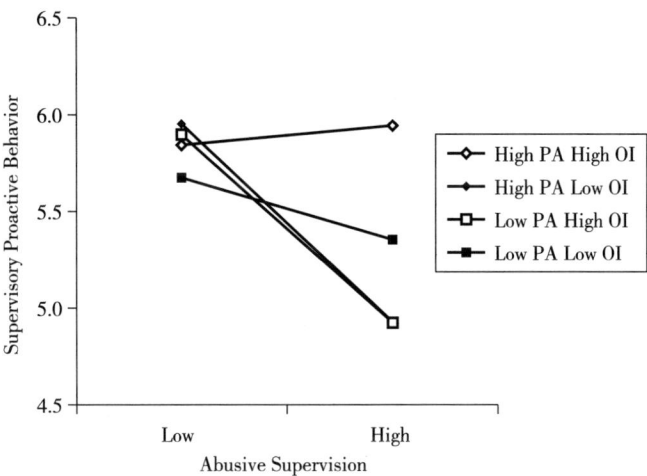

FIGURE 4.3 Plot of the Three-Way Interaction on Supervisory Proactive Behavior in Study 2

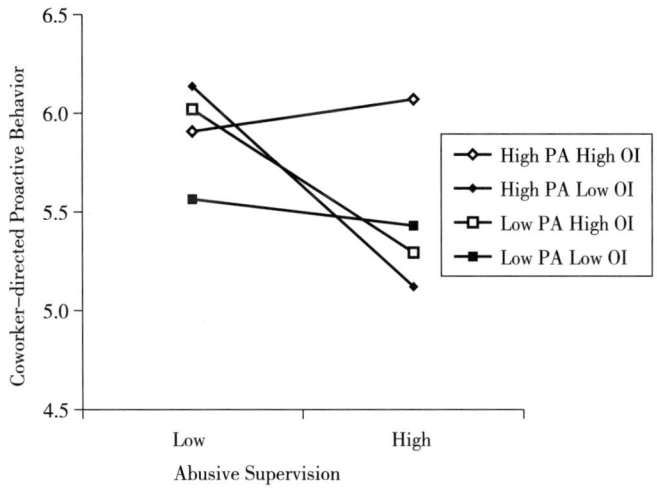

FIGURE 4.4 Plot of the Three-Way Interaction on Coworker-directed Proactive Behavior in Study 2

4.3.5 Discussion

The purpose of this study was to confirm the findings in Study 1 as well as address its limitations. Results from a sample of 226 employee-supervisor dyads in a Chinese transportation company showed that, abusive supervision was negatively related to supervisory proactive behavior, but was not significantly related to organizational and coworker-directed proactive behaviors. Moreover, the three-way interactive effect of abusive supervision, organizational identification and positive affectivity was all significantly related to three forms of proactive behaviors. However, three interactive patterns were not exactly the same for organizational, supervisory and coworker-directed proactive behaviors.

The study had several limitations. First, this study used a cross-sectional design, which made it difficult to infer the causal relationships between abusive supervision and subordinate proactive behaviors. Second, because the data were collected from all Chinese employees, the generalizabililty of the findings across all cultures was still obscure. Third, the measure of supervisory proactive behavior was adopted from the voice literature, thus limited the content of initiative actions an employee could actually conduct towards supervisors. Finally, the contents of the three forms of proactive behaviors were asymmetric and might interfere with the results.

In Chapter 5, I provide an overview of the finding of two studies, discuss the implications, limitations, and suggest possible future research directions.

5 GENERAL DISCUSSION

5.1 Overview of Findings

Proactive behavior is a type of behavior that is "self-initiated, anticipatory action aimed at changing either the situation or oneself" (Bindl & Parker, 2011, p. 1). It can be beneficial for organizational competitiveness and individuals' well-being. Not surprisingly, researchers have started to investigate the predictors of employee proactive behavior. However, recent studies have called for further and thorough investigation of the role of abusive supervision in the proactivity literature (Burris et al., 2008; Parker et al., 2010), and discovered divergent results for the moderating role of organizational identification in the stress process (Decoster et al., 2013; Haslam et al., 2009; Reilly, 1994; Xu et al., 2015). Addressing these, the present study has based on transactional model of stress (Lazarus & Folkman, 1984, 1987) and explored how and when abusive supervision influences subordinates' proactive behaviors. In general, supervisory abuse is perceived as a workplace stressor, and depletes subordinates' physical and cognitive resources. Moreover, how individuals appraise and react to stressful situations should depend not only on their beliefs and goals, but on their dispositions. Therefore, I hypothesized that abusive supervision was negatively related to subordinates' proactive behavior and then it interacted with organizational identification and trait positive affectivity to influence proactive behavior. Two field studies were conducted to test these hypotheses.

The findings are summarized as follows. First, supervisory abuse had direct and negative effects on employee general proactivity and supervisor-directed proactivity. It was found in Study 1 that abusive supervision was negatively associated with personal initiative and in Study 2 that abusive supervision was significantly linked to supervisory proactive behavior. Contrary to my expectation, abusive supervision did not have a significant impact on subordinates' organization- and coworker-directed proactive behaviors. One possible explanation is that abused subordinates are most likely to reduce favorable behaviors and retaliate toward the harm doers such as their supervisors.

Second, the data showed that the three-way interaction of abusive supervision, organizational identification and positive affectivity significantly predicted subordinates' proactivity in terms of general proactivity, organization-, supervisor- and coworker-directed proactive behaviors. As expected, when organizational identification was low and positive affectivity was high, the association between abusive supervision and proactivity was the most detrimental. Surprisingly, it was found that in Study 2, when organizational identification was high and positive affectivity was low, supervisory abuse had a significant and negative impact on supervisor- and coworker-directed proactive behaviors. One possible reason is the target issue is salient. When performing supervisory and coworker-directed proactive behaviors, identification toward organization may lose its buffering role as a resource pool, especially for subordinates with low PA, because these subordinates will not be capable of integrating diverse organizational resources and overcoming the risks from supervisors and coworkers.

5.2　Theoretical Implications

　　The results of this study contribute to the previous literature in several ways. First, this research has extended proactivity literature by investigating the impact of abusive supervision on proactive behavior. Previous reviews all noted that positive supervisory leadership had an effect on subordinates' proactive behavior, and that workplace stressors including job stressors all had an influence on employee proactivity (for reviews, see Bind & Parker, 2011; Parker et al., 2010). More relevantly, three studies examined the relationship between abusive supervision, a typical workplace stressor, and subordinate proactivity in terms of voice to supervisor or organization (Burris et al., 2008; Li et al., 2009; Rafferty & Restubog, 2011). However, the generalizability of these studies to other types of individual proactivity was limited. Burris et al. (2008) called for more research on the predicting role of abusive supervision on proactive behaviors toward coworkers. Therefore, by providing empirical evidence for the assumptions that abusive supervision had an influence on general and targeted proactive behaviors, this research further extended the nomological network of proactive behavior and turned researchers' attention to the destructive side of leadership and social stressors.

　　Second, this study contributes to the literature by taking an interactional perspective to explore the relationship between abusive supervision and employee proactivity. A review by Bindl and Parker (2011) acknowledged that situational and individual antecedents interacted to influence proactivity. This research follows this trend and becomes the first to explore the moderating role of subordinates' personal characteristics (i.e., beliefs, affective disposition) on the impact of abusive supervision. Furthermore, this study offers a possible explanation for the nonsignificant associations between supervisor undermining, similar to abusive supervision, and proactivity (Kammeyer-Muller et al., 2013; Ng & Feldman, 2013). Specifically, such relationship may be contingent on individual characteristics such as identification with organization and positive affectivity.

Third, this research advances our understanding of the role of organizational identification in the proactivity literature. Scholars have argued that organizational identification has a positive influence on employee suggestion-making behaviors (e.g., Fuller et al., 2006; Liu et al., 2010; Morrison et al., 2011; Yang & Liu, 2014). My findings showed that organizational identification was positively associated with supervisor-rated personal initiative in Study 1, but was not significantly related to supervisor-rated proactive behaviors directed at organization, supervisor and coworkers in Study 2. I call for more research to explore the impact of organizational identification since it is an individual's fundamental belief. Further, researchers have also argued that individuals who identify with their organization are likely to tie their positive self-concept to organization's successes, and behave in a way that will achieve organization's goals, thereby dampening the influence of unfavorable personal values and situational factors (Lipponen, Bardi & Haapamäki, 2008; Tangirala & Ramanujam, 2008). These empirical findings in this study showed that organizational identification was ineffective in weakening the effect of negative situational antecedents on supervisor- and coworker-directed proactive behaviors when individuals were low in positive affectivity.

Fourth, these findings shed some lights on the inconsistent results of the moderating effect of organizational identification on how individuals responded to workplace stressors. A study by Decoster et al. (2013) argued that when an individual identified with the organization, he or she would perceive work was meaningful. Therefore, under the condition of supervisory abuse, identified employees would respond in a more positive way. Based on a sample of 134 employee-supervisor dyads, they found support for this buffering hypothesis. However,

Reilly (1994) used a sample of 645 hospital nurses, and reported that employees who more strongly identified with their employing organizations were more likely to experience the adverse effects of workplace stressors, compared to those who less strongly identified. Furthermore, Harris and colleagues (2007) hypothesized that employees who valued their work in the organizations might spend extra effort dealing with their abusive supervisor, and as a consequence, reacted more negatively. Using a sample of 209 employees from an automotive corporation, they found support for this prediction. These divergent results might be due to moderators. This study extends the literature on abusive supervision and proactive behavior by identifying positive affectivity as a boundary condition of the moderating effect of organizational identification on how individuals react to stressful situations.

Fifth, my findings that the associations between the stressor and proactive behaviors rely on a combination of individual beliefs and dispositions further the literature on moderators of the influence of abusive supervision (e. g., Mawritz, Dust & Resick, 2014; Mitchell & Ambrose, 2007; Tepper, Duffy & Shaw, 2001). Abusive supervisors belittle subordinates, humiliate them and criticize them in front of others. Abused subordinates who lowly identify with their organizations may respond quite negatively, especially when they have an overall sense of happiness. Thus, when positive affectivity is high, abusive supervision may be too stressful for those low on organizational identification. Combining the beliefs of being a member of the organization with the aversive influence of supervisory abuse can make them feel too sensitive and reluctant to perform proactive behavior (Hochwarter et al., 2003). On the other hand, for those with low levels of positive affectivity and organizational identification, abused subordinates may not respond too intensively and act too passively. In contrast, employees who highly identify with their organizations receive more support from others, and take the organizational goals as their own, thereby suffering a lower destructive effect of abusive supervisors, no matter their positive affectivity level. In Study 1, for individuals with high organizational identification, abusive supervision is not significantly related to personal initiative of subordinates, no matter their positive affectivity level. I also found a similar result for subordinates' organizational proactive behavior in Study 2.

Finally, this study contributes to the proactivity literature by gaining an in-depth understanding of the association between positive affectivity and proactivity. Levels of positive affectivity—defined as the extent to which employees generally experienced positive feelings (Gilmore, Hu, Wei, Tetrick & Zaccaro, 2013; Watson & Clark, 1992) —affected how an individual reacts to supervisory impact in association with proactivity, thereby responding to a critical question in the proactive behavior literature (Bindl & Parker, 2012). Furthermore, it has been argued that positive affectivity has a positive effect on proactivity, but I propose that the tendency to experience positive feelings may make employees respond intensively to stressors and constraints in the focal organization, thereby producing a disadvantage in the proactive pursuits of bringing changes. As such, positive affectivity could actually be detrimental to proactivity.

5.3 Practical Implications

Like other studies, this study has several implications for managers and organizations. In an era of fierce competition, managers need proactive employees to anticipate the future and take initiative to bring about change. Research has reported that organizational proactivity was positively related with financial performance (Aragón-Correa, Hurtado-Torres, Sharma & García-Morales, 2008). Hence, it is important for managers to promote proactivity in their organizations. To begin with, my findings suggest that organizations should be aware of the negative influence of abusive supervision on subordinates' general proactivity and should spend all efforts reducing the occurrence of abusive supervisory behaviors. Research has suggested that supervisors' stress and depression are related to subordinates' perceptions of abusive supervision (Burton, Hoolber & Scheuer, 2012; Tepper, Duffy, Henle & Lambert, 2006). Thus, supervisors could find ways to release their negative feelings and manage their own negative behaviors properly. Organizations should appropriately allocate resources, and provide adequate trainings for supervisors in terms of abuse-prevention, emotion management and other behavioral tools (Aryee et al., 2008; Zhang, Kwan, Zhang & Wu, 2012).

Moreover, extant research has indicated that perceptions of organizational injustice, violations of psychological contracts and manager's abusive behaviors can cause supervisors to perform abusive behaviors (Hoobler & Brass, 2006; Liu, Liao & Loi, 2012; Tepper et al., 2006). Organizations should create a just work climate, consider supervisors' needs and encourage all organizational members to act as positive role models. Recent research has also revealed that relationship conflict leads to abusive supervision (Tepper, Moss & Duffy, 2011). Therefore, organizations should encourage leaders and employees to utilize appropriate strategies such as mediation and reconciliation to deal with relationship conflict. Additionally, managers should be encouraged to constantly monitor themselves and seek feedbacks from employees so that they can gauge how employees perceive their managerial styles.

Second, my results have implications for Human Resources activities that aim to enhance organizational identification. Although existing literature suggests that strengthening organizational identification helps increase employee proactive behavior (e.g., Fuller, Hester, Barnett, Frey, Relyea & Beu, 2006; Lipponen et al., 2008; Yang & Liu, 2014), this research suggests a contingency approach. On the one hand, individuals high on positive affectivity show the lowest levels of proactivity when organizational identification is low and abusive supervision is high. On the other hand, individuals high on positive affectivity show more proactive behaviors than their low counterparts when organizational identification is high and abusive supervision is high. Therefore, organizations calling for more proactivity from employees should pay attention to employees' levels of positive affectivity before deciding whether to strengthen organizational identification. Generally speaking, increasing organizational identification is likely to be more effective when combined with a match of abusive supervisors and individuals high on positive affectivity.

Finally, although the literature has shown that positive affectivity has a positive influence on individual proactive behavior (Bindl & Parker, 2012; Den Hartog & Belschak, 2007), this research points out that it can be detrimental in the process of proactive pursuit. Thus, organizations should take such complex impact of affective personality into consideration. While individuals with high positive affectivity are generally more likely to have energy and take initiative, the results indicate that they may respond more strongly to negative environmental stimuli.

5.4 Limitations

Similarly, the current research has some limitations. First, firm conclusions about causality cannot be drawn from this study. For instance, the results of Study 1 suggest that abusive supervision significantly decreases personal initiative. I have assumed this direction of causality, which is in line with theoretical suggestions in the studies on proactive behavior (e.g., Burris et al., 2006). However, it is possible that an employee's bad performance on proactive behavior motivates his or her supervisor to exhibit abusive actions accordingly. This would be in consistency with some of the extant literature (Frese & Fay, 2001) which notes that supervisors may feel threatened by their subordinates' proactive actions. On the contrary, supervisors may react to a high level of proactive behaviors from subordinates by providing fewer advancement opportunities, offering less emotional support, holding different values from the subordinates, and so on. High levels of proactivity do not necessarily drive a leader to engage in abusive behaviors toward subordinates. One way to clarify the direction of causality of the model for future research would be to conduct an experimental or longitudinal study.

Second, the results may be affected by common method bias because the analyses regarding the key variables of two studies are conducted using measures procured at a single point. Although the results of the CFA provided support for the distinctiveness of variables, this study could not completely rule out the common method bias. In particular, common method bias could lead to the high correlations between the predictors, especially pertaining to the three foci of proactive behavior in Study 2. However, several scholars (Podsakoff, MacKenzie & Podsakoff, 2012; Siemsen, Roth & Oliveira, 2010) have suggested that significance of interaction effects cannot be affected by common method variance, revealing that the three-way moderating effect of abusive supervision, organizational identification and positive affectivity on proactive behaviors are not its artifacts. I also suggest that future research may better cope with this common method bias problem by collecting data at different points in time (Podsakoff, MacKenzie, Lee & Podsakoff, 2003).

Third, all three foci of proactive behaviors in Study 2 were rated by supervisors. Albeit it is reasonable to have supervisors report organizational and supervisory proactive behaviors, it may raise concerns over accuracy for supervisors to rate proactive behavior toward the coworkers. This type of proactive behavior is likely to be more accurately perceived and evaluated by coworkers rather than supervisors, who are subject to the halo effect (Nisbett & Wilson, 1977). Although some researchers have demonstrated that supervisor-reported behaviors toward peers were highly correlated with those reported by peers (e.g., Liu et al.,

2010), the results of this study should be interpreted cautiously. I suggest that future research measures this construct by using data sources such as supervisors and coworkers at the same time.

Fourth, following the above limitation, the items for proactive behavior toward different targets may also vary in terms of content of proactive actions. To some degree, I have tried to control for the content of proactive behavior by using actions that are mostly symmetric in content but different in target (e.g., idea generation and suggestion is part of all three foci of proactive behavior; optimizing the organization of work and taking over tasks is included as proactive behavior in different type). Yet, such symmetry in content was not procured for all items and future research should include additional items to guarantee further symmetry.

Fifth, although most of the scales used (except supervisory proactive behavior) in this study were well-developed and tested in Chinese context, one scale was suffered from low internal consistency problem. For example, the alpha internal consistency/reliability coefficient for the measure of positive affectivity in Study 1 was 0.60. This low value was not unusual (Choi, 2007; Grant, 2013; Hui, Wong & Tjosvold, 2007). Moreover, Carmines and Zeller (1979) suggested that the acceptable criterion for use in research was 0.60. One reason for the low reliability estimate might be that this construct was measured by Thompson's (2007) 5-item positive affectivity scale. Such highly shortened measure can reduce reliability (Credé, Harms, Nierhorster & Gaye-Valentine, 2012). I suggest that future studies use more comprehensive measures of positive affectivity than those included in the I-PANAS-SF.

Sixth, the means of abusive supervision reported in my samples are relatively low (M=1.80, Study 1; M=1.45, Study 2). However, my findings are consistent with previous studies showing the means of abusive supervision ranging from low, such as 1.26 (Tepper et al., 2011) and 1.36 (Tepper, Carr, Breaux, Geider, Hu & Hua, 2009), to high, such as 2.63 (Wang et al., 2012) and 2.70 (Biron, 2010). Further, as the interactional effect among abusive supervision, organizational identification and positive affectivity for proactive behaviors has been found significant, I feel confident that these low means of abusive supervision may raise little concern for data analysis.

Last but not least, data were obtained from one organization in China, so the generalizability of the results to other industries and countries was limited. Tepper (2007) has already suggested that "it is worth acknowledging that in industries where a primary objective is to remold the identity of new recruits, organizations may sanction the use of hostile behavior on the part of supervisors against their direct reports". A recent review posited that this industry effect of abusive supervision still remained unknown (Martinko et al., 2013). Likewise, the results of this study may also differ in countries because China is a high power distance society. The negative effects of abusive supervision in this sample may be even stronger in other countries like the USA, which is a low power distance society. Future cross-cultural research may examine the boundary conditions of abusive supervision.

5.5 Future Research Directions

This study aims to investigate how the complex interaction of abusive supervision, organizational identification and positive affectivity influences employee proactivity from the transactional model of stress. More effort should be put into this respect.

First, my findings are limited to one type of destructive leadership-abusive supervision. Future research may examine a broader range of interpersonal mistreatments, including actions from supervisors that are physical and not hostile. For example, certain types of interpersonal mistreatment, such as social undermining and workplace incivility, sustainably harm employees, which may induce low resources and poor social exchange relationships in the workplace (Duffy, Ganster, Shaw, Johnson & Pagon, 2006; Scott et al., 2013). It is of theoretical and empirical importance to examine whether the relationships between nontraditional interpersonal mistreatment and different proactive behaviors are dissimilar.

Second, this is one of the first studies that emphasizes the detrimental role of negative supervisory behaviors in predicting subordinates' proactivity. Following the logic of transactional model of stress, other types of job-related stressors such as time urgency may also have an effect. Future research should follow this direction and conduct systematic examination.

Third, unlike the adverse effect of abusive supervision, it is of vital importance to further explore other workplace factors which play a facilitating role in encouraging employees' proactive behaviors. For instance, leader humility, as a new but interesting topic, has been found to lead to followers' high levels of engagement, satisfaction, and commitment. All of these attitudes could result in high frequencies of proactive behaviors. However, no research thus far has explored such a relationship.

A fourth valuable direction is to identify the influences of identification with different targets or groups. I focus in this study on the role of identification with an organization in employees' proactive pursuits under the condition of abusive supervision. Identification with other social groups or targets may impact individuals' proactive reactions to stressors as well (e.g., identification with the work group, supervisor, and coworker-coworker relationship). Future work should explore the influences of these factors.

Fifth, although I drew from the transactional model of stress to explain the underlying mechanism of the influence of the complex interplay between abusive supervision, organizational identification and positive affectivity on proactive behavior, I did not directly test the intermediating mechanism. Other theoretical perspectives are also possible. I call for more sophisticated research to investigate the potential mediators.

Another possible direction is to examine the cause-effect relationships between abusive supervision and subordinate proactive behavior. The present study used a cross-sectional research design, and thus, the cause-effect relations could not be inferred from the findings. Future research should employ a longitudinal or experimental research design to examine the causal relationships contained in this study.

5.6 Conclusions

Along with the advent of knowledge-based economic era, employees are playing an increasingly important role in Chinese organizations. Instead of passively accepting assigned tasks, employees can initiatively or proactively fulfill their responsibilities. Such proactivity has been argued to be effective to help organizations survive and thrive in the complex environment. Therefore, organizations have tried their best to encourage employees to take the initiative. For example, managers took measures to create an innovative climate so that employees had stronger confidence for performing proactive actions (Chen et al., 2013). Moreover, leaders gave followers the freedom to work on their own, and thus, their followers might set proactive goals and then result in more taking charge behaviors (Martin et al., 2013).

With the discovery of such emphasis on positive situational antecedents, this study suggests that in reality, situations will not always be positive and then argues that abusive supervision is a possible inhibitory factor. In addition, the detrimental effect of such factor will be dependent on a combination of organizational and individual personal factors. Employing the transactional model of stress, the present study proposes a model in which abusive supervision negatively impacts proactive behavior, and abusive supervision, organizational identification and positive affectivity interact to impact subordinates' proactive behavior in such a way that when organizational identification is low and positive affectivity is high, the relationship between abusive supervision and proactive behavior is the most negative.

This study tested the hypotheses based on two field sub-studies (Study 1: dentists; Study 2: employees in transportation industry). The findings showed that abusive supervision was significantly and negatively related to general proactivity and supervisor-directed proactivity. Furthermore, the present data indicated that abusive supervision, organizational identification and positive affectivity interactively influenced subordinate proactivity in terms of general proactivity, organization-, supervisor-, and coworker-directed proactive behaviors. When organizational identification was low and positive affectivity was high, the detrimental effect of abusive supervision on proactive was the strongest.

The findings in the present study have significant implications for organizations which implement certain practices in order to promote proactive behaviors. On the one hand, organizational managers can learn how to better undermine the negative effect of abusive supervision and boost proactive behaviors. On the other hand, the leaders should keep in mind that when encouraging proactive actions, they need to take a holistic view of the measures, and be sure of the mutual reinforcement of them.

REFERENCES

Adams, J. S. (1963). Toward an understanding of inequity. Journal of Abnormal and Social Psychology, 67: 422-436.

Adams, J. S. (1965). Inequity in social exchange. In Berkowitz, L. (Ed.). Advances in experimental social psychology. New York: Academic Press.

Aiken, L. S., & West, S. G. (1991). Multiple regression: Testing and interpreting interactions. Thousand Oaks, CA: Sage.

Ambrose, M. L., & Kulik, C. T. (1999). Old friends, new faces: Motivation in the 1990s. Journal of Management, 25: 231-292.

Aragón-Correa, J. A., Hurtado-Torres, N., Sharma, S., & García-Morales, V. J. (2008). Environmental strategy and performance in small firms: A resource-based perspective. Journal of Environmental Management, 86 (1): 88-103.

Aryee, S., Chen, Z. X., Sun, L., & Debrah, Y. A. (2007). Antecedents and outcomes of abusive supervision: Test of a trickle-down model. Journal of Applied Psychology, 92: 191-201.

Aryee, S., Sun, L. Y., Chen, Z. X., & Debrah, Y. A. (2008). Abusive supervision and contextual performance: The mediating role of emotional exhaustion and the moderating role of work unit structure. Management and Organization Review, 4 (3): 393-411.

Ashford, S. J., Blatt, R., &Vande Walle, D. (2003). Reflections on the looking glass: A review of research on feedback-seeking behavior in organizations. Journal of Management, 29 (6): 773-799.

Ashford, S. J., & Cummings, L. L. (1983). Feedback as an individual resource: Personal strategies of creating information. Organizational Behavior and Human Performance, 32: 370-398.

Ashford, S. J., & Cummings, L. L. (1985). Proactive feedback seeking: The instrumental use of the information environment. Journal of Occupational Psychology, 58: 67-79.

Ashford, S. J., Rothbard, N. P., Piderit, S. K., & Dutton, J. E. (1998). Out on a limb: The role of context and impression management in selling gender-equity issues. Administrative Science Quarterly, 43 (1): 23-57.

Ashforth, B. E., Harrison, S. H., & Corley, K. G. (2008). Identification in organizations: An examination of four fundamental questions. Journal of Management, 34 (3): 325-374.

Ashforth, B. E., & Mael, F. (1989). Social identity theory and the organization. Academy of Management Review, 14: 20-39.

Avey, J. B., Wernsing, T. S., & Palanski, M. E. (2012). Exploring the process of ethical leadership: The mediating role of employee voice and psychological ownership. Journal of Business Ethics, 107: 21-34.

Axtell, C. M., Holman, D. J., Unsworth, K. L., Wall, T. D., & Waterson, P. E. (2000). Shopfloor innovation: Facilitating the suggestion and implementation of ideas. Journal of Occupational and Organizational Psychology, 73 (3): 265-285.

Baer, M., & Frese, M. (2003). Innovation is not enough: Climates for initiative and psychological safety, process innovations, and firm performance. Journal of Organizational Behavior, 24 (1): 45-68.

Bandura, A. (1982). Self-efficacy mechanism in human agency. American Psychologist, 37: 122-147.

REFERENCES

Bandura, A. (1997). Self-efficacy: The exercise of control. New York: Freeman.

Barsade, S., & Gibson, D. E. (2007). Why does affect matter in organizations? Academy of Management Perspectives, 21: 36–59.

Bateman, T. S., & Crant, J. M. (1993). The proactive component of organizational behavior: A measure and correlates. Journal of Organizational Behavior, 14 (2): 103–118.

Belschak, F. D., & Den Hartog, D. N. (2010). Pro-self, pro-social, and pro-organizational foci of proactive behavior: Differential antecedents and consequences. Journal of Occupational and Organizational Psychology, 83: 475–498.

Bentler, P. M. (1990). Latent variable structural models for separating specific from general effects. In L. Sechrest, E. Perrin, & J. Bunker (Eds.), Research methodology: Strengthening causal interpretations of non-experimental data (DHHS Publication No. PHS 90-3454). Washington, DC: US Department of Health and Human Services.

Bindl, U. K., & Parker, S. K. (2011). Proactive work behavior: Forward thinking and change-oriented action in organizations. In S. Zedeck (Eds.), APA handbook of industrial and organizational psychology, Washington, DC: American Psychological Association.

Bindl, U. K., & Parker, S. K. (2012). Affect and employee proactivity: A goal-regulatory perspective. In Ashkanasy, N. M., Härtel, C. E. J., Zerbe, W. J., (Eds.). Experiencing and managing emotions in the workplace (Research on Emotion in Organizations). Emerald Group Publishing Limited.

Biron, M. (2010). Negative reciprocity and the association between perceived organizational ethical values and organizational deviance. Human Relations, 63: 875–897.

Blader, S. L., & Tyler, T. R. (2009). Testing and extending the group engagement model: Linkages between social identity, procedural justice, economic outcomes, and extra-role behavior. Journal of Applied Psychology, 94: 445-464.

Blickle, G., Meurs, J. A., Wihler, A., Ewen, C., Plies, A. & Günther, S. (2013). The interactive effects of conscientiousness, openness to experience, and political skill on job performance in complex jobs: The importance of context. Journal of Organizational Behavior, 34: 1145-1164.

Bolger, N., & Amarel, D. (2007). Effects of social support visibility on adjustment to stress: Experimental evidence. Journal of Personality and Social Psychology, 92 (3): 458-475.

Bolger, N., & Zuckerman, A. (1995). A framework for studying personality in the stress process. Journal of Personality and Social Psychology, 69: 890-902.

Bolger, N., Zuckerman, A., & Kessler, R. C. (2000). Invisible support and adjustment to stress. Journal of Personality and Social Psychology, 79 (6): 953-961.

Brislin, R. W. (1980). Translation and content analysis of oral and written materials. In H. C. Triandis & J. W. Berry (Eds.), Handbook of cross-cultural psychology. Boston, MA: Allyn & Bacon.

Brockner, J. (1988). Self-esteem at work: Research, theory, and practice. Lexington, MA: Lexington Books.

Brown, M. E., Treviño, L. K., & Harrison, D. A. (2005). Ethical leadership: A social learning perspective for construct development and testing. Organizational Behavior and Human Decision Processes, 97: 117-134.

Browne, M. W., & Cudeck, R. (1993). Alternative ways of assessing model fit. In K. Bollen, & J. S. Long (Eds.), Testing structural equations models, 136-162. Newbury Park, CA: Sage.

Burris, E. R., Detert, J. R., & Chiaburu, D. S. (2008). Quitting before leaving: The mediating effects of psychological attachment and detachment on voice. Journal of Applied Psychology, 93 (4): 912-922.

REFERENCES

Burton, J. P., Hoolber, J. M., & Scheuer, M. L. (2012). Supervisor workplace stress and abusive supervision: The buffering effect of exercise. Journal of Business Psychology, 27: 271-279.

Carless, S. A., & Bernath, L. (2007). Antecedents of intent to change careers among psychologists. Journal of Career Development, 33 (3): 183-200.

Carmines, E. G., & Zeller, R. A. (1979). Reliability and validity assessment. Beverly Hills, CA: Sage.

Carver, C. S., & Scheier, M. F. (1982). Control theory: A useful conceptual framework for personality-social, clinical, and health psychology. Psychological Bulletin, 92 (1): 111-135.

Chen, G., Farh, J. -L., Campbell-Bush, E. M., Wu, Z., & Wu, X. (2013). Teams as innovative systems: multilevel motivational antecedents of innovation in R&D teams. Journal of Applied Psychology, 98 (6): 1018-1027.

Chen, Z., Lam, W., & Zhong, J. A. (2007). Leader-member exchange and member performance: A new look at individual-level negative feedback-seeking behavior and team-level empowerment climate. Journal of Applied Psychology, 92 (1): 202-212.

Cheng, J., Lu, K., Chang, Y., & Johnstone, S. (2012). Voice Behavior and work engagement: The moderating role of supervisor-attributed motives. Asia Pacific Journal of Human Resources, 51 (1): 81-102.

Choi, J. N. (2007). Change-oriented organizational citizenship behavior: Effects of work environmental characteristics and intervening psychological processes. Journal of Applied Psychology, 28: 467-484.

Crant, J. M. (2000). Proactive behavior in organizations. Journal of Management, 26 (3): 435-462.

Crant, J. M., & Bateman, T. S. (2000). Charismatic leadership viewed from above: The impact of proactive personality. Journal of Organizational Behavior, 21: 63-75.

Credé, M., Harms, P. D., Nierhorster, S., & Gaye-Valentine, A.

(2012). An evaluation of the consequences of using short measures of the Big Five personality traits. Journal of Personality and Social Psychology, 102: 874-888.

Csikszentmihalyi, M. (1988). The flow experience and its significance for human psychology. In M. Csikszentmihalyi & I. S. Csikszentmihalyi (Eds.), Optimal experience: Psychological studies of flow in consciousness, 15–35. Cambridge, UK: Cambridge University Press.

De Cremer, D. (2003). How self–conception may lead to inequality: Effect of hierarchical roles on the equality rule in organizational resource-sharing tasks. Group and Organization Management, 28: 282-302.

Deci, E. L., & Ryan, R. M. (2000). The "what" and "why" of goal pursuits: Human needs and the self-determination of behavior. Psychological Inquiry, 11: 227-268.

Decoster, S., Camps, J., Stouten, J., Vandevyvere, L., & Tripp, T. M. (2013). Standing by your organization: The impact of organizational identification and abusive supervision on followers' perceived cohesion and tendency to gossip. Journal of Business Ethics, 118: 623-634.

Den Hartog, D. N., & Belschak, F. D. (2007). Personal initiative, commitment and affect at work. Journal of Occupational and Organizational Psychology, 80: 601-622.

Den Hartog, D. N., & Belschak, F. D. (2012). When does transformational leadership enhance employee proactive behavior? The role of autonomy and role breadth self-efficacy. Journal of Applied Psychology, 97 (1): 194-202.

Detert, J. R., & Burris, E. R. (2007). Leadership behavior and employee voice: Is the door really open? Academy of Management Journal, 50: 869-884.

Duffy, M. K., Ganster, D. C., & Shaw, J. D. (1998). Positive affectivity and negative outcomes: The role to tenure and job satisfaction. Journal of Applied Psychology, 83: 950-959.

Duffy, M. K., Ganster, D. C., Shaw, J. D., Johnson, J. L., & Pagon, M. (2006). The social context of undermining behavior at work. Organizational Behavior and Human Decision Processes, 101: 105–126.

Dutton, J. E., Ashford, S. J., O'Neill, R. M., & Lawrence, K. A. (2001). Moves that matter: Issue selling and organizational change. Academy of Management Journal, 44 (4): 716–736.

Dutton, J. E., Dukerich, J. M., & Harquail, C. V. (1994). Organizational images and member identification. Administrative Science Quarterly, 39 (2): 239–263.

Edmondson, A. (1999). Psychological safety and learning behavior in work teams. Administrative Science Quarterly, 44: 350–383.

Einarsen, S., Aasland, M. S., & Skogstad, A. (2007). Destructive leadership behavior: A definition and conceptual model. The Leadership Quarterly, 18: 207–216.

Epitropaki, O., & Martin, R. (2005). The moderating role of individual differences in the relation between transformational/transactional leadership perceptions and organizational identification. The Leadership Quarterly, 16: 569–589.

Farndale, E., Van Ruiten, J., Kelliher, C., & Hope-Hailey, V. (2011). Perceived employee voice on organizational commitment: An exchange perspective. Human Resource Management, 50 (1): 113–129.

Fay, D., & Frese, M. (2001). The concept of personal initiative: An overview of validity studies. Human Performance, 14 (1): 97–124.

Fay, D., & Sonnentag, S. (2002). Rethinking the effects of stressors: A longitudinal study on personal initiative. Journal of Occupational Health Psychology, 7 (3): 221–234.

Folkman, S., Lazarus, R. S., Gruen, R. J., & DeLongis, A. (1986). Appraisal, coping, health status, and psychological symptoms. Journal of Personality and Social Psychology, 50: 571–579.

Frazier, M. L., & Bowler, W. M. (2012). Voice climate, supervisor undermining, and work outcomes: A group-level examination. Journal of Management, 41 (3): 841-863.

Fredrickson, B. L. (1998). What good are positive emotions? Review of General Psychology, 2 (3): 300-319.

Fredrickson, B. L. (2001). The role of positive emotions in positive psychology: The broaden-and-build theory of positive emotions. American Psychologist, 56 (3): 218-226.

Frese, M., & Fay, D. (2001). Personal initiative: An active performance concept for work in the 21st century. In Staw, B. M., & Sutton, R. I. (Eds.), Research in organizational behavior, 23: 133-187.

Frese, M., Fay, D., Hilburger, T., Leng, K., & Tag, A. (1997). The concept of personal initiative: Operationalization, reliability and validity in two German samples. Journal of Occupational and Organizational Psychology, 70: 139-161.

Frese, M., Garst, H., & Fay, D. (2007). Making things happen: Reciprocal relationships between work characteristics and personal initiative in a four-wave longitudinal structural equation model. Journal of Applied Psychology, 92 (4): 1084-1102.

Frese, M., Kring, W., Soose, A., & Zempel, J. (1996). Personal initiative at work: Differences between East and West Germany. Academy of Management Journal, 39 (1): 37-63.

Frese, M., Teng, E., & Wijnen, C. J. D. (1999). Helping to improve suggestion systems: Predictors of making suggestions in companies. Journal of Organizational Behavior, 20: 1139-1155.

Frisch, J. U., Häusser, J. A., van Dick, R., & Mojzisch, A. (2014). Making support work: The interplay between social support and social identity. Journal of Experimental Social Psychology, 55: 154-161.

Fritz, C., Yankelevich, M., Zarubin, A., & Barger, P. (2010). Happy, healthy, and productive: The role of detachment from work during nonwork time. Journal of Applied Psychology, 95 (5): 977–983.

Fuchs, S., & Edwards, M. R. (2011). Predicting pro-change behavior: The role of perceived organizational justice and organizational identification. Human Resource Management Journal, 22 (1): 39–59.

Fuller, J. B., Hester, K., Barnett, T., Frey, L., Relyea, C., & Beu, D. (2006). Perceived external prestige and internal respect: New insights into the organizational identification process. Human Relations, 59 (6): 815–846.

Fuller, B. Jr., & Marler, L. E. (2009). Change driven by nature: A meta-analytic review of the proactive personality literature. Journal of Vocational Behavior, 75 (3): 329–345.

Fuller, B. Jr., Marler, L. E., & Hester, K. (2006). Promoting felt responsibility for constructive change and proactive behavior: Exploring aspects of an elaborated model of work design. Journal of Organizational Behavior, 27: 1089–1120.

Fuller, B. Jr., Marler, L. E., & Hester, K. (2012). Bridge building within the province of proactivity. Journal of Organizational Behavior, 33: 1053–1070.

Ganster, D., & Schaubroeck, J. (1991). Work stress and employee health. Journal of Management, 17: 235–271.

George, J. M. (1992). The role of personality in organizational life: Issues and evidence. Journal of Management, 18: 185–213.

Gilboa, S., Shirom, A., Fried, Y., & Cooper, C. (2008). A meta-analysis or work demand stressors and job performance: Examining main and moderating effects. Personnel Psychology, 61: 227–271.

Gilmore, P. L., Hu, X. X., Wei, F., Tetrick, L. E., & Zaccaro, S. J. (2013). Positive affectivity neutralizes transformational leadership's influence on creative performance and organizational citizenship behaviors. Journal of Organizational Behavior, 34: 1061–1075.

Gong, Y., Cheung, S. Y., Wang, M., & Huang, J. C. (2012). Unfolding the proactive process for creativity: Integration of the employee proactivity, information exchange, and psychological safety perspectives. Journal of Management, 38 (5): 1611-1633.

Goussinsky, R. (2011). Does customer aggression more strongly affect happy employees? The moderating role of positive affectivity and extraversion. Motivation & Emotion, 35: 220-234.

Grant, A. M. (2007). Relational job design and the motivation to make a prosocial difference. Academy of Management Review, 32: 393-417.

Grant, A. M. (2007). Rocking the boat but keeping it steady: The role of emotion regulation in employee voice. Academy of Management Journal, 56 (6): 1703-1723.

Grant, A. M., & Ashford, S. J. (2008). The dynamics of proactivity at work. Research in Organizational Behavior, 28: 3-34.

Grant, A. M., & Rothbard, N. P. (2013). When in doubt, seize the day? Security values, prosocial values, and proactivity under ambiguity. Journal of Applied Psychology, 98 (5): 810-819.

Grant, A. M., & Sumanth, J. J. (2009). Mission possible? The performance ofprosocially motivated employees depends on manager trustworthiness. Journal of Applied Psychology, 94 (4): 927-944.

Greenberg, J., & Colquitt, J. A. (2005). The handbook of organizational justice. Mahwah, NJ: Erlbaum.

Griffin, R. W., & Lopez, Y. P. (2005). "Bad behavior" in organizations: A review and typology for future research. Journal of Management, 31: 988-1005.

Griffin, M. A., Neal, A., & Parker, S. K. (2007). A new model of work role performance: Positive behavior in uncertain and interdependent contexts. Academy of Management Journal, 50: 327-347.

Hacker, W. (1985). Activity: A fruitful concept in industrial psychology.

In M. Frese & J. Sabini (Eds.), Goal-directed behavior: The concept of action in psychology, 262-283. Hillsdale, NJ: Erlbaum.

Hackman, J. R., & Oldham, G. R. (1976). Motivation through the design of work: Test of a theory. Organizational Behaviour and Human Performance, 16: 250-279.

Hakanen, J. J., Perhoniemi, R., & Toppinen - Tanner, S. (2008). Positive gain spirals at work: From job resources to work engagement, personal initiative and work-unit innovativeness. Journal of Vocational Behavior, 73: 78-91.

Harris, K. J., Lambert, A. & Harris, R. B. (2013). HRM effectiveness as a moderator of the relationships between abusive supervision and technology work overload and job outcomes for technology end users. Journal of Applied Social Psychology, 43: 1686-1695.

Harris, K. J., Kacmar, K. M., & Zivnuska, S. (2007). An investigation of abusive supervision as a predictor of performance and the meaning of work as a moderator of the relationship. The Leadership Quarterly, 18: 252-263.

Harvey, P., Stoner, J., Hochwarter, W., & Kacmar, C. (2007). Coping with abusive supervision: The neutralizing effects of ingratiation and positive affect on negative employee outcomes. The Leadership Quarterly, 18: 264-280.

Haslam, S. A., Jetten, J., & Waghorn, C. (2009). Social identification, stress and citizenship in teams: A five - phase longitudinal study. Stress and Health, 25: 21-30.

Haslam, S. A., & Reicher, S. D. (2006). Stressing the group: Social identity and the unfolding dynamics of responses to stress. Journal of Applied Psychology, 91: 1037-1052.

Hobman, E. V., Restubog, S. L. D. R., Bordia, P. & Tang, R. L. (2009). Abusive supervision in advising relationships: Investigating the role of social support. Applied Psychology: An International Review, 58 (2): 233-256.

Hochwarter, W. A., Kiewitz, C., Castro, S. L., Perrewé, P. L., & Ferris, G. R. (2003). Positive affectivity and collective efficacy as moderators of the relationship between perceived politics and job satisfaction. Journal of Applied Social Psychology, 33: 1009-1035.

Hofmann, D. A., & Gavin, M. B. (1998). Centering decisions in hierarchical linear models: Theoretical and methodological implications for organizational science. Journal of Management, 23: 623-641.

Hoobler, J., & Brass, D. (2006). Abusive supervision and family undermining as displaced aggression. Journal of Applied Psychology, 91: 1125-1133.

Hornung, S., & Rousseau, D. M. (2007). Active on the job-proactive in change: How autonomy at work contributes to employee support for organizational change. Journal of Applied Behavioral Science, 43 (4): 401-426.

Hornung, S., Rousseau, D. M., & Glaser, J. (2008). Creating flexible work arrangements through idiosyncratic deals. Journal of Applied Psychology, 93 (3): 655-664.

Howell, J. M., & Boies, K. (2004). Champions of technological innovation: The influence of contextual knowledge, role orientation, idea generation, and idea promotion on champion emergence. The Leadership Quarterly, 15 (1): 123-143.

Hoyle, R. H. (1995). Structural equation modeling: Concepts, issues, and applications. Thousand Oaks, CA: SAGE.

Hsiung, H. H. (2012). Authentic leadership and employee voice behavior: A multi-level psychological process. Journal of Business Ethics, 107: 349-361.

Huang, J. (2012). Be proactive as empowered? The role of trust in one's supervisor in psychological empowerment, feedback seeking, and job performance. Journal of Applied Social Psychology, 42: 103-127.

Hui, C., Wong, A. & Tjosvold, D. (2007). Turnover intention and performance in China: The role of positive affectivity, Chinese values, perceived organizational support, and constructive controversy. Journal of Occupational and Organizational Psychology, 80: 735-751.

Ilgen, D., & Hollenbeck, J. (1991). The structure of work: Job design and roles. In Dunnette, M. D., & Hough, L. M. (Eds.), Handbook of industrial and organizational psychology. Palo Alto: Consulting Psychologists Press.

Ivancevich, J. M., & Donnelly, J. H. Jr. (1974). A study of role clarity and need for clarity for three occupational groups. Academy of Management Journal, 17: 28-36.

James, L. R., Mulaik, S. A., & Brett, J. M. (2006). A tale of two methods. Organizational Research Methods, 9: 233-244.

Janssen, O., & Gao, L. (2013). Supervisory responsiveness and employee self-perceived status and voice behavior. Journal of Management, 1-19.

Janssen, O., & Van Yperen, N. W. (2004). Employees' goal orientation, the quality of leader-member exchange, and the outcomes of job performance and job satisfaction. Academy of Management Journal, 47 (3): 368-384.

Judge, T. A. (1993). Does affective disposition moderate the relationship between job satisfaction and voluntary turnover? Journal of Applied Psychology, 78: 395-401.

Kammeyer-Mueller, J., Wanberg, C., Rubenstein, A., & Song, Z. (2013). Support, undermining, and newcomer socialization: Fitting in during the first 90 days. Academy of Management Journal, 56 (4): 1104-1124.

Kanfer, R., Wanberg, C. R., & Kantrowitz, T. M. (2001). Job search and employment: A personality-motivational analysis and meta-analytic review. Journal of Applied Psychology, 86: 837-855.

Kaplan, S., Bradley, J. C., Luchman, J. N., & Haynes, D. (2009). On the role of positive and negative affectivity in job performance: A meta-analytic investigation. Journal of Applied Psychology, 94 (1): 162-176.

Kelloway, E. K. (1996). Common practices in structural equation model-ling. In C. L. Cooper & I. T. Robertson (Eds.), International review of industrial and organizational psychology. Chichester, England: Wiley.

Kipnis, D., Schmidt, S. M., & Wilkinson, I. (1980). Intraorganizational influence tactics: Explorations in getting one's way. Journal of Applied Psychology, 65: 440-452.

Lam, C. F., Spreitzer, G., & Fritz, C. (2013). Too much of a good thing: Curvilinear effect of positive affect on proactive behaviors. Journal of Organizational Behavior, 35: 530-546.

Larsen, R. J., & Ketelaar, T. (1991). Personality and susceptibility to positive and negative emotional states. Journal of Personality and Social Psychology, 41: 132-140.

Latham, G. P., & Pinder, C. C. (2005). Work motivation theory and research at the dawn of the twenty-first century. Annual Review of Psychology, 56: 495-516.

Lazarus, R. S. (1995). Psychological stress in the workplace. In R. Crandall, & P. L. Perrewe (Eds.), Occupational stress. Washington, DC: Taylor and Francis.

Lazarus, R. S., & Folkman, S. (1984). Stress, appraisal, and coping. New York: Springer.

Lazarus, R. S., & Folkman, S. (1987). Transactional theory and research on emotions and coping. European Journal of Personality, 1: 141-169.

Le Pine, J. A., Podsakoff, N. P., & Le Pine, M. A. (2005). A meta-analytic test of the challenge stressor hindrance stressor framework: An explanation for inconsistent relationships among stressors and performance. Academy of Management Journal, 48 (5): 764-775.

Le Pine, J. A., & Van Dyne, L. (1998). Predicting voice behavior in work groups. Journal of Applied Psychology, 83: 853-868.

Leung, K., Huang, K., Su, C., & Lu, L. (2011). Curvilinear relationships between role stress and innovative performance: Moderating effects of perceived support for innovation. Journal of Occupational and Organizational Psychology, 84: 741-758.

Li, N., Chiaburu, D. S., Kirkman, B. L., & Xie, Z. (2013). Spotlight on the followers: An examination of moderators of relationships between transformational leadership and subordinates' citizenship and taking charge. Personnel Psychology, 66: 225-260.

Li, R., Ling, W., & Liu, S. (2009). The mechanisms of how abusive supervision impacts on subordinates' voice behavior. Acta Psychologica Sinica, 41 (12): 1189-1202.

Lian, H., Ferris, D. L., & Brown, D. J. (2012). Does taking the good with the bad make things worse? How abusive supervision and leader-member exchange interact to impact need satisfaction and organizational deviance. Organizational Behavior and Human Decision Processes, 117: 41-52.

Liang, J., Farh, C. I. C., & Farh, J. (2012). Psychological antecedents of promotive and prohibitive voice: A two-wave examination. Academy of Management Journal, 55 (1): 71-92.

Liden, R. C., Sparrowe, R. T., & Wayne, S. J. (1997). Leader-member exchange theory: The past and potential for the future. In Ferris, G. R. (Eds.), Research in personnel and human resources management. US: Elsevier Science/JAI Press.

Lipponen, J., Bardi, A., & Haapamäki, J. (2008). The interaction between values and organizational identification in predicting suggestion-making at work. Journal of Occupational and Organizational Psychology, 81: 241-248.

Liu, W., Tangirala, S., & Ramanujam, R. (2013). The relational antecedents of voice targeted at different leaders. Journal of Applied Psychology, 98 (5): 841-851.

Liu, D., Liao, H., & Loi, R. (2012). The dark side of leadership: A three-level investigation of the cascading effect of abusive supervision on employee creativity. Academy of Management Journal, 55: 1187-1212.

Liu, W., Zhu, R., & Yang, Y. (2010). I warn you because I like you: Voice behavior, employee identifications, and transformational leadership. The Leadership Quarterly, 189-202.

Locke, E. A. (1968). Towards a theory of task motivation and incentives. Organizational Behavior and Human Performance, 3: 157-189.

Locke, E. A., & Latham, G. P. (2002). Building a practically useful theory of goal setting and task motivation: A 35-year odyssey. American Psychologist, 57: 705-717.

Love, M. S., & Dustin, S. (2014). An investigation of coworker relationships and psychological collectivism on employee propensity to take charge. The International Journal of Human Resource Management, 25 (9): 1208-1226.

Madrid, H. P., Paterson, M. G., Birdi, K. S., Leiva, P. L., & Kausel, E. E. (2014). The role of weekly high-activated positive mood, context, and personality in innovative work behavior: A multilevel and interactional model. Journal of Organizational Behavior, 35: 234-256.

Mael, F., & Ashforth, B. E. (1992). Alumni and their alma mater: A partial test of the reformulated model of organizational identification. Journal of Organizational Behavior, 13: 103-123.

Maisel, N. C., & Gable, S. L. (2009). The paradox of received social support: The importance of responsiveness. Psychological Science, 20 (8): 928-932.

Martin, S. L., Liao, H., & Campbell, E. M. (2013). Directive versus empowering leadership: A field experiment comparing impacts on task proficiency and proactivity. Academy of Management Journal, 56 (5): 1372-1395.

Martinko, M. J., Harvey, P., Brees, J. R., & Mackey, J. (2013). A review of abusive supervision research. Journal of Organizational Behavior, 34: 120-137.

Maslach, C., Schaufeli, W. B., & Leiter, M. P. (2001). Job burnout. Annual Review of Psychology, 52: 397-422.

Maslow, A. H. (1954). Motivation and personality. New York: Harper & Row.

Mawritz, M. B., Dust, S. B., & Resick, C. J. (2014). Hostile climate, abusive supervision, and employee coping: Does conscientiousness matter? Journal of Applied Psychology, 99 (4): 737-747.

McClelland, D. C. (1961). The achieving society. Princeton, NJ: Van Nostrand.

McClelland, D. C. (1971). Assessing human motivation. New York: General Learning Press.

Mitchell, M. S., & Ambrose, M. L. (2007). Abusive supervision and workplace deviance and the moderating effects of negative reciprocity beliefs. Journal of Applied Psychology, 92 (4): 1159-1168.

Morrison, E. W. (2002). Newcomers' relationships: The role of social network ties during socialization. Academy of Management Journal, 45: 1149-1160.

Morrison, E. W. (2006). Doing the job well: An investigation of pro-social rule breaking. Journal of Management, 32: 5-28.

Morrison, E. W., & Phelps, C. C. (1999). Taking charge at work: Extra-role efforts to initiate workplace change. Academy of Management Journal, 42 (4): 403-419.

Morrison, E. W., Wheeler-Smith, S. L., & Kamdar, D. (2011). Speaking up in groups: A cross-level study of group voice climate and voice. Journal of Applied Psychology, 96 (1): 183-191.

Nandkeolyar, A. K., Shaffer, J. A., Li, A., Ekkirala, S., & Bagger, J. (2014). Surviving an abusive supervisor: The joint roles of conscientiousness and coping strategies. Journal of Applied Psychology, 99 (1): 138-150.

Ng, T. W., & Feldman, D. C. (2012). Age and innovation-related behavior: The joint moderating effects of supervisor undermining and proactive personality. Journal of Organizational Behavior, 34: 583-606.

Ng, T. W., & Feldman, D. C. (2013). Changes in perceived supervisor embeddedness: Effects on employees' embeddedness, organizational trust, and voice behavior. Personnel Psychology, 66: 645-685.

Nisbett, R. E., & Wilson, T. D. (1977). The halo effect: Evidence for unconsciousalteration of judgments. Journal of Personality and Social Psychology, 35 (4): 250-256.

Ohly, S., & Fritz, C. (2007). Challenging the status quo: What motivates proactive behavior? Journal of Occupational and Organizational Psychology, 80 (4): 623-629.

Ohly, S., & Fritz, C. (2010). Work characteristics, challenge appraisal, creativity and proactive behavior: A multi-level study. Journal of Organizational Behavior, 31: 543-565.

Ohly, S., Sonnentag, S., & Pluntke, F. (2006). Routinization, work characteristics and their relationships with creative and proactive behaviors. Journal of Organizational Behavior, 27 (3): 257-279.

Organ, D. W. (1990). The motivational basis of organizational citizenship behavior, in B. M. Staw & L. L. Cummings (Eds.), Research in organizational behavior. Greenwich, CT: JAI Press.

Parker, S. K., Bindl, U. K., & Strauss, K. (2010). Making things happen: A model of proactive motivation. Journal of Management, 36 (4): 827-856.

Parker, S. K., & Collins, C. G. (2010). Taking stock: Integrating and differentiating multiple proactive behaviors. Journal of Management, 36 (3): 633-662.

Parker, S. K., Wall, T. D., & Jackson, P. R. (1997). "That's not my job": Developing flexible employee work orientations. Academy of Management Journal, 40: 899-929.

Parker, S. K., Williams, H. M., & Turner, N. (2006). Modeling the antecedents of proactive behavior at work. Journal of Applied Psychology, 91

(3): 636-652.

Parkinson, B., Totterdell, P., Briner, R. B., & Reynolds, S. (1996). Changing moods. The psychology of moods and mood regulation. Essex: Addison Wesley Longman.

Pervin, L. A. (1989). Persons, situations, interactions: The history of a controversy and a discussion of theoretical models. Academy of Management Review, 14: 350-360.

Pieterse, A. N., Van Knippenberg, D., Schippers, M., & Stam, D. (2010). Transformational and transactional leadership and innovative behavior: The moderating role of psychological empowerment. Journal of Organizational Behavior, 31: 609-623.

Podsakoff, P. M., MacKenzie, S. B., Lee, J. Y., & Podsakoff, N. P. (2003). Common method biases in behavioral research: A critical review of the literature and recommended remedies. Journal of Applied Psychology, 88: 879-903.

Podsakoff, P. M., MacKenzie, S. B., & Podsakoff, N. P. (2012). Sources of method bias in social science research and recommendations on how to control it. Annual Review of Psychology, 63: 539-569.

Premeaux, S. F., & Bedeian, A. G. (2003). Breaking the silence: The moderating effects of self-monitoring in predicting speaking up in the workplace. Journal of Management Studies, 1537-1562.

Priesemuth, M., Schminke, M., Ambrose, M. L., & Folger, R. (2014). Abusive supervision climate: A multiple-mediation model of its impact on group outcomes. Academy of Management Journal, 57 (5): 1513.

Rafferty, A. E., & Restubog, S. L. D. (2011). The influence of abusive supervisors on followers' organizational citizenship behaviors: The hidden costs of abusive supervision. British Journal of Management, 22: 270-285.

Rank, J., Carsten, J. M., Unger, J. M., & Spector, P. E. (2007). Proactive customer service performance: Relationships with individual, task, and leadership variables. Human Performance, 20 (4): 363-390.

Rank, J., Nelson, N. E., Allen, T. D., & Xu, X. (2009). Leadership predictors of innovation and task performance: Subordinates' self-esteem and self-presentation as moderators. Journal of Occupational and Organizational Psychology, 82: 465-489.

Raub, S., & Liao, H. (2012). Doing the right thing without being told: Joint effects of initiative climate and general self-efficacy on employee proactive customer service performance. Journal of Applied Psychology, 97 (3): 651-667.

Raudenbush, S. W., & Bryk, A. S. (2002). Hierarchical linear models: Applications and data analysis methods. Thousand Oaks, CA: Sage.

Reilly, N. P. (1994). Exploring a paradox: Commitment as a moderator of the stressor-burnout relationship. Journal of Applied Social Psychology, 24: 397-414.

Riketta, M. (2005). Organizational identification: A meta-analysis. Journal of Vocational Behavior, 66: 358-384.

Rioux, S. M., & Penner, L. A. (2001). The causes of organizational citizenship behavior: A motivational analysis. Journal of Applied Psychology, 86: 1306-1314.

Russell, J. A. (2003). Core affect and the psychological construction of emotion. Psychological Review, 110 (1): 145-172.

Salanova, M., & Schaufeli, W. B. (2008). A cross-national study of work engagement as a mediator between job resources and proactive behavior. The International Journal of Human Resource Management, 19 (1): 116-131.

Schaubroeck, J., & Jones, J. R. (2000). Antecedents of workplace emotional labor dimensions and moderators of their effects on physical symptoms. Journal of Organizational Behavior, 21: 163-183.

Scott, S. G., & Bruce, R. A. (1994). Determinants of innovative behavior: A path model of individual innovation in the workplace. Academy of Management Journal, 37: 580-607.

Scott, K. L., Restubog, S. L. D., & Zagenczyk, T. J. (2013). A social exchange-based model of the antecedents of workplace exclusion. Journal of Applied Psychology, 98 (1): 37-48.

Seibert, S. E., Crant, M. J., & Kraimer, M. L. (1999). Proactive personality and career success. Journal of Applied Psychology, 84: 416-427.

Seibert, S. E., Kraimer, M. L., & Crant, J. M. (2001). What do proactive people do? A longitudinal model linking proactive personality and career success. Personnel Psychology, 54 (2): 845-874.

Shaw, J. D., Duffy, M. K., Abdulla, M., & Singh, R. (2000). The moderating role of positive affectivity: Empirical evidence from bank employees in the United Arab Emirates. Journal of Management, 26: 139-154.

Siemsen, E., Roth, A., & Oliveira, P. (2010). Common method bias in regression models with linear, quadratic, and interaction effects. Organizational Research Methods, 13: 456-476.

Sonnentag, S. (2003). Recovery, work engagement, and proactive behavior: A new look at the interface between nonwork and work. Journal of Applied Psychology, 88 (3): 518-528.

Speier, C., & Frese, M. (1997). Generalized self-efficacy as a mediator and moderator between control and complexity at work and personal initiative: A longitudinal field study in East Germany. Human Performance, 10 (2): 171-192.

Spitzmuller, M., & Van Dyne, L. (2013). Proactive and reactive helping: Contrasting the positive consequences of different forms of helping. Journal of Organizational Behavior, 34: 560-580.

Spreitzer, G. M. (1995). An empirical test of a comprehensive model of intrapersonal empowerment in the workplace. American Journal of Community Psychology, 23: 601-629.

Strauss, K., Griffin, M. A., & Rafferty, A. E. (2009). Proactivity directed toward the team and organization: The role of leadership, commitment and role-breadth self-efficacy. British Journal of Management, 20: 279-291.

Tajfel, H. (1978). Differentiation between social groups: Studies in the social psychology of intergroup relations. London: Academic Press.

Tajfel, H., & Turner, J. C. (1979). An integrative theory of intergroup conflict. In M. J. Hatch & M. Schultz (Eds.), Organizational identity: A reader, 56-65. New York, NY: Oxford University Press.

Tangirala, S., & Ramanujam, R. (2008). Exploring non-linearity in employee voice: The effects of personal control and identification. Academy of Management Journal, 51: 1189-1203.

Tepper, B. J. (2000). Consequences of abusive supervision. Academy of Management Journal, 43 (2): 178-190.

Tepper, B. J. (2007). Abusive supervision in work organizations: Review, synthesis, and directions for future research. Journal of Management, 33: 261-289.

Tepper, B. J., Carr, J. C., Breaux, D. M., Geider, S., Hu, C., & Hua, W. (2009). Abusive supervision, intentions to quit, and employees' workplace deviance: A power/dependence analysis. Organizational Behavior and Human Decision Processes, 109: 156-167.

Tepper, B. J., Duffy, M. K., Henle, C. A., & Lambert, L. S. (2006). Procedural injustice, victim precipitation, and abusive supervision. Personnel Psychology, 59: 101-123.

Tepper, B. J., Duffy, M. K., & Shaw, J. D. (2001). Personality moderators of the relationship between abusive supervision and subordinates' resistance. Journal of Applied Psychology, 86: 974-983.

Tepper, B. J., Moss, S. E., & Duffy, M. K. (2011). Predictors of abusive supervision: Supervisor perceptions of deep-level dissimilarity, relationship conflict, and subordinate performance. Academy of Management Journal, 54: 279-294.

Thomas, J. P., Whitman, D. S., & Viswesvaran, C. (2010). Employee proactivity in organizations: A comparative meta-analysis of emergent proactive constructs. Journal Occupational and Organizational Psychology, 83: 275-300.

Thompson, E. R. (2007). Development and validation of an internationally reliable short-form of the Positive and Negative Affect Schedule (PANAS). Journal of Cross-Cultural Psychology, 38: 227-242.

Tornau, K., & Frese, M. (2012). Construct clean-up in proactivity research: A meta-analysis on the nomological net of work-related proactivity concepts and their incremental validities. Applied Psychology: An International Review, 62 (1): 44-96.

Tröster, C., & van Knippenberg, D. (2012). Leader openness, nationality dissimilarity, and voice in multinational management teams. Journal of International Business Studies, 43: 591-613.

Tuckey, M., Brewer, N., & Williamson, P. (2002). The influence of motives and goal orientation on feedback seeking. Journal of Occupational and Organizational Psychology, 75 (2): 195-216.

Turner, J. C. (1982). Towards a cognitive redefinition of the social group. In H. Tajfel (Eds.), Social identity and intergroup relations, 15-40. Cambridge: Cambridge University Press.

Turner, J. C. (1985). Social categorization and the self-concept: A social cognitive theory of group behavior. In E. J. Lawler (Eds.), Advances in group processes: Theory and research, 77-122. Greenwich, CT: JAI Press.

Unsworth, K. L., & Parker, S. K. (2003). Proactivity and innovation: Promoting a new workforce for the new workplace. In D. Holman, T. D. Wall, C. W. Clegg, P. Sparrow, & A. Howard (Eds.), The new workplace: A guide to the human impact of modern working practices, 175-196. Chichester, England: Wiley.

Van Dick, R., & Wagner, U. (2002). Social identification among school teachers: Dimensions, foci, and correlates. European Journal of Work and Organizational Psychology, 11: 129-149.

Van Dyne, L., Cummings, L. L., & McLean Parks, J. (1995). Extra-role behaviors: In pursuit of construct and definitional clarity. InL. L., Cummings, & B. M. Staw, (Eds.). Research in organizational behavior, 17: 215-285. Greenwich, CT: JAI Press.

Van Dyne, L., & Le Pine, J. A. (1998). Helping and voice extra-role behaviors: Evidence of construct and predictive validity. Academy of Management Journal, 41 (1): 108-119.

VanEerde, W., & Thierry, H. (1996). Vroom's expectancy models and work-related criteria: A meta-analysis. Journal of Applied Psychology, 81: 575-586.

Venkataramani, V., & Tangirala, S. (2010). When and why do central employees speak up? An examination of mediating and moderating variables. Journal of Applied Psychology, 95 (3): 582-591.

Vroom, V. H. (1964). Work and motivation. New York: Wiley.

Walumbwa, F. O., Cropanzano, R., & Hartnell, C. A. (2009). Organizational justice, voluntary learning behavior, and job performance: A test of the mediating effects of identification and leader-member exchange. Journal of Organizational Behavior, 30: 1103-1126.

Walumbwa, F. O., & Schaubroeck, J. (2009). Leader personality traits and employee voice behavior: Mediating roles of ethical leadership and work group psychological safety. Journal of Applied Psychology, 94 (5): 1275-1286.

Wanberg, C. R., & Kammeyer-Mueller, J. D. (2000). Predictors and outcomes of proactivity in the socialization process. Journal of Applied Psychology, 85 (3): 373-385.

Wang, W., Mao, J., Wu, W., & Liu, J. (2012). Abusive supervision and workplace deviance: The mediating role of interactional justice and the moderating role of power distance. Asia Pacific Journal of Human Resources, 50: 43-60.

REFERENCES

Warr, P., & Fay, D. (2001). Short report: Age and personal initiative at work. European Journal of Work and Organizational Psychology, 10 (3): 343–353.

Watson, D., & Clark, L. A. (1984). Negative affectivity: The disposition to experience aversive emotional states. Psychological Bulletin, 96: 465–490.

Watson, D., & Clark, L. A. (1992). On traits and temperament: General andspecific factors of emotional experience and their relation to the five-factor model. Journal of Personality, 60: 441–476.

Watson, D., Clark, L. A., & Tellegen, A. (1988). Development and validation of brief measures of positive and negative affect—The PANAS scales. Journal of Personality and Social Psychology, 54 (6): 1063–1070.

Watson, D., & Tellegen, A. (1985). Toward a consensual structure of mood. Psychological Bulletin, 98: 219–235.

Wegge, J., Schuh, S. C., & van Dick, R. (2012). "I feel bad", "We feel good"? Emotions as a driver for personal and organizational identity and organizational identification as a resource for serving. Stress and Health, 28: 123–136.

Weigl, M., Müller, A., Hornung, S., Zacher, H., & Angerer, P. (2013). The moderating effects of job control and selection, optimization, and compensation strategies on age-work ability relationship. Journal of Organizational Behavior, 34: 607–628.

Williams, J. S., Gray, L. N., & von Broembsen, M. H. (1976). Proactivity and reinforcement: The contingency of social behavior. Small Group Behavior, 7: 317–330.

Wu, C. H., Parker, S. K., & de Jong, J. P. J. (2011). Need for cognition as an antecedent of individual innovation behavior. Journal of Management, 40 (6): 1511–1534.

Xu, E., Huang, X, Lam, C. K., & Miao, Q. (2012). Abusive supervision and work behaviors: The mediating role of LMX. Journal of Organizational

Behavior, 33: 531-543.

Xu, Q., Xi, M., Zhao, S., & Li, F. (2015). Abusive supervision and subordinate silence: A cross-level investigation of the role of HPWS. Paper to be presented at the Annual SIOP Conference, Vancouver, BC, Canada.

Yang, L., Johnson, R. E., Zhang, X., Spector, P. E., & Xu, S. (2013). Relations of interpersonal unfairness with counterproductive work behavior: The moderating role of employee self-identity. Journal of Business Psychology, 28: 189-202.

Yang, Q., & Liu, M. (2014). Ethical leadership, organizational identification and employee voice: Examining moderated mediation process in the Chinese insurance industry. Asia Pacific Business Review, 20 (2): 231-248.

Yuan, F., & Woodman, R. W. (2010). Innovative behavior in the workplace: The role of performance and image outcome expectations. Academy of Management Journal, 53 (2): 323-342.

Zellars, K. L., Perrewe, P. L., Hochwarter, W. A., & Anderson, K. S. (2006). The interactive effects of positive affect and conscientiousness on strain. Journal of Occupational Health Psychology, 11 (3): 281-289.

Zellars, K. L., Tepper, B. J., & Duffy, M. K. (2002). Abusive supervision and subordinates' organizational citizenship behavior. Journal of Applied Psychology, 87 (6): 1068-1076.

Zhang, Y., Huai, M., & Xie, Y. (2014). Paternalistic leadership and employee voice in China: A dual process model. The Leadership Quarterly, 26 (1): 25-36.

Zhang, H., Kwan, H. K., Zhang, X., & Wu, L. Z. (2012). High core self-evaluators maintain creativity: A motivational model of abusive supervision. Journal of Management, 40 (4): 1151-1174.

APPENDIX A

A Summary of Empirical Studies on the Relationship between Supervisory Antecedents and Proactivity

Authors	Antecedents	Mediators/Moderators	Outcomes	Main Findings
Avey et al. (2012)	Ethical behavior		Voice	Supervisor's ethical behavior was positively related to voice.
Axtell et al. (2000)	Team leader support		Suggestions; Implementation	Team leader support was not significantly related to these outcomes.
Belschak & Den Hartog (2010)	Transformational leader behavior (TFL)		Organizational, interpersonal and personal proactive behaviors	TFL was positively related to organizational and interpersonal proactive behaviors, but not related to personal proactive behavior.

续表

Authors	Antecedents	Mediators/Moderators	Outcomes	Main Findings
Burris, Detert & Chiaburu (2008)	Abusive supervision; LMX	**Mediators:** Affective commitment; Intention to leave	Voice to supervisor	Intention to leave mediates relations between leaderships and voice, whereas affective commitment is not a mediator of leadership-voice relations.
Chen &Aryee (2007)	Delegation	**Mediators:** Perceived insider status; OBSE **Moderator:** Traditionality	Innovative behavior	OBSE and perceived insider status mediated the relationship between delegation and innovative behavior. Traditionality moderated the relationships between delegation and OBSE and perceived insider status.
Chen, Lam & Zhong (2007)	LMX	**Moderators:** Sense of empowerment; Empowerment climate	Negative feedback-seeking behavior (NFB)	LMX was positively related to NFB. Team empowerment climate was positively related to subordinates' sense of empowerment, which moderated the effects of LMX on NFB.
Chiaburu & Baker (2006)	Supervisor output and process control		Taking charge	Output control significantly predicted taking charge; Process control was notrelated to taking charge.

APPENDIX A

Authors	Antecedents	Mediators/Moderators	Outcomes	Main Findings
Den Hartog & Belschak (2012)	TFL	**Moderators:** Job autonomy; Role breadth self-efficacy	Personal initiative; Prosocial proactive behavior	TFL was positively related to three proactive concepts. TFL, job autonomy and self-efficacy interactively influence proactive behavior.
Hsiung (2012)	Authentic behavior	**Mediators:** LMX, Positive mood **Moderator:** Procedural justice climate	Voice	LMX and positive mood mediated the relationship between authentic leader behaviors and voice. Procedural justice climate moderates the relations between LMX, positive mood and voice.
Huang (2012)	Psychological empowerment	**Mediators:** Trust in supervisor, feedback seeking	Job performance	Psychological empowerment is positively related to feedback-seeking behavior via trust in supervisor. Feedback-seeking behavior mediates the relation between trust in supervisor and job performance.
Janssen & Gao (2013)	Supervisory responsiveness	**Mediator:** Self-perceived status; **Moderator:** Self-efficacy	Voice	Self-perceived status mediated the relationship between supervisory responsiveness and voice. The indirect relation through self-perceived status was more pronounced when self-efficacy for voice was higher rather than lower.

续表

Authors	Antecedents	Mediators/Moderators	Outcomes	Main Findings
Janssen & VanYperen (2004)	LMX		Innovative job performance	LMX was positively linked to innovative job performance.
Kammeyer-Mueller, Wanberg, Rubenstein & Song (2013)	Supervisor undermining; Coworker undermining	**Mediators:** Hedonic tone; Proactive socialization	Work proactivity (organizational)	Supervisory undermining is not related to work proactivity.
Li, Ling & Liu (2009)	Abusive supervision	**Mediators:** POS; Psychological safety **Moderators:** Perceived supervisory status	Promotive voice; Prohibitive voice (Work unit)	Abusive supervision had a negative influence on both voice behaviors. Specifically, abusive supervision's negative effect on promotive voice was mediated by POS, while its effect on prohibitive voice was mediated by POS and psychological safety. Abusive supervision was more strongly associated with POS when subordinates perceived higher supervisory status. Meanwhile, the indirect effects of abusive supervision on voice mediated by POS or psychological safety were stronger when perceived supervisory status was higher.

APPENDIX A

续表

Authors	Antecedents	Mediators/Moderators	Outcomes	Main Findings
Liu, Tangirala & Ramanujam (2013)	LMX, SMX (Exchange between employee and skip-level leader)	**Moderators:** LLX (Exchange between direct supervisor and skip-level leader), SMX, LMX	Voice to the direct supervisor; Voice to the skip-level leader	The choice of a particular leader as a target was affected by the quality of the dyadic relationship between that leader and the employee. The relation between voice to the direct supervisor and LMX was stronger when LXX was stronger. The relation between voice to the skip-level leader and SMX was more positive when LLX was weaker.
Liu, Zhu & Yang (2010)	TFL	**Mediators:** Social identification; Personal identification	Speaking up and out	Social identification partially mediated the relationship between TFL and speaking out. Personal identification fully mediated the relation between TFL and speaking up.
Martin, Liao & Campbell (2013)	Directive and empowering behaviors	**Moderator:** Initial satisfaction with supervisor	Proactive behavior	Empowering leadership increased proactive behaviors; Directive leadership enhanced proactive behaviors for work units that were highly satisfied with their supervisors, whereas empowering leadership had stronger effects on both core task proficiency and proactive behaviors for work units that were less satisfied with their supervisors.

续表

Authors	Antecedents	Mediators/Moderators	Outcomes	Main Findings
Ng & Feldman (2012)	Supervisor undermining	**Moderators**: Age, proactive personality	Innovation behavior	Supervisor undermining was not related to innovation-related behavior.
Ng & Feldman (2013)	Supervisor embeddedness	**Mediators**: employees' own embeddedness organizational trust	voice	Supervisor embeddedness was directly related to employees' own embeddedness over time. Organizational trust mediated the relationship between supervisor embeddedness and employees' own embeddedness over time. Organizational trust and employee embeddedness were both related to employees' voice behavior over time.
Ohly, Sonnentag & Plunke (2006)	Supervisor support		Personal initiative	Supervisor support was significantly and positively related to personal initiative.
Parker, Williams & Turner (2006)	Supportive supervision		Proactive behavior	Supportive supervision is not related to proactive behavior.
Pieterse, Van Knippenberg, Schippers & Stam (2010)	TFL; transactional leadership	**Moderators**: Psychological empowerment (PE)	Innovative behavior	TFL is positively related to innovative behavior only when PE is high. Transactional leadership was negatively related to innovation only under high PE.

APPENDIX A

续表

Authors	Antecedents	Mediators/Moderators	Outcomes	Main Findings
Premeaux & Bedeian (2003)	Trust in supervisor	**Moderator:** Self-monitoring	Speaking up	Low self-monitors, in comparison to high self-monitors, spoke up more often as trust in supervisor increased.
Rafferty & Restubog (2011)	Abusive supervision	**Mediators:** Meaning of work; OBSE Interactional justice	Prosocial voice (Organization)	Abusive supervision was significantly negatively associated with followers' perceptions of interactional justice, which in turn was negatively associated with supervisor-rated prosocial voice behaviours.
Rank et al. (2007)	TFL; Participative leadership		Proactive service performance	Participative leadership was significantly related to PSP, but TFL was not related to proactive service performance.
Rank, Nelson, Allen & Xu (2009)	TFL; Transactional leadership	**Moderators:** OBSE; Self-presentation	Innovative behavior	TFL positively predicted both criteria; Transactional leadership negatively predicted innovation. TFL related more strongly to innovation for subordinates low in OBSE.
Scott & Bruce (1994)	Leader role expectations; LMX	**Mediators:** Support for innovation; Resource supply	Innovative behavior	Leader role expectations are positively related to innovative behavior. Support for innovation and resource supply mediated the relation between LMX and innovation.

续表

Authors	Antecedents	Mediators/Moderators	Outcomes	Main Findings
Tröster & van Knippenberg (2012)	Supervisor openness	**Mediators:** Affective commitment	Supervisor-directed voice	Supervisors of multinational teams profit more from the local know-how of employees from under represented nationalities when they are open to their ideas, and when they have the same nationality.
Walumbwa & Schaubroeck (2009)	Ethical behaviors	**Mediators:** Psychological safety	Voice	The relation between ethical leadership and voice was partially mediated by psychological safety.
Yang & Liu (2014)	Ethical behaviors	**Mediators:** Organizational identification (OI); **Moderators:** Organizational trust	Voice	OI fully mediates the positive influence of ethical leadership on employee voice. Organization trust moderates the relationship between OI and employee voice.
Yuan & Woodman (2010)	Supervisor relationship quality	**Mediators:** Image gains and positive performance outcomes	Innovative behavior	Supervisor relationship quality was positively associated with innovative behavior. Expected image gains and positive performance outcomes mediated the relationship.

APPENDIX A

续表

Authors	Antecedents	Mediators/Moderators	Outcomes	Main Findings
Zhang, Huai & Xie (2014)	Paternalistic leadership	**Mediators:** LMX; Status judgement	Voice	Authoritarian leaders reduce voice by reducing their status judgment. Benevolent leaders encourage voice by enhancing both LMX and status judgment. Moral leaders positively influence voice mainly through LMX processes.

APPENDIX B

Scale Items

Organizational proactive behavior

1. This employee personally takes the initiative to suggest ideas for solutions for company problems.

这个员工会主动提出解决公司问题的思路或想法。

2. This employee personally takes the initiative to acquire new knowledge that will help the company.

这个员工会主动汲取对公司有用的新知识。

3. This employee personally takes the initiative to optimize the organization of work to further organizational goals.

这个员工会主动完善工作流程,以实现公司目标。

Supervisory proactive behavior

1. This employee communicates his or her opinions about work issues to me even if his or her opinion is different, and I disagree with him or her.

即使他的观点和我的不同,这个员工也会与我交流关于工作问题的看法。

2. This employee gives constructive suggestions to me to improve my work.

这个员工会向我提出有效的建议，以改进我的工作。

3. If I made mistakes in my work, this employee would point them out and help me correct them.

如果我在工作中犯了错误，这个员工会主动指出来，并帮助我改正。

4. This employee speaks to me with new ideas for projects.

这个员工会告诉我关于公司项目运营的新思路，或者改进项目运营的新主意。

Coworker-directed proactive behavior

1. This employee personally takes the initiative to share knowledge with colleagues.

这个员工会主动与他的同事分享工作经验。

2. This employee personally takes the initiative to take over colleagues' tasks when needed even though she/he is not obligated to.

尽管事不关己，这个员工也会主动帮助其他同事完成任务。

3. This employee personally takes the initiative to help orient new colleagues.

这个员工会主动帮助新同事适应公司环境。

4. This employee personally takes the initiative to help colleagues with developing or implementing new ideas.

这个员工会主动帮助其他同事完善和实施新的想法。

Personal initiative

1. This employee actively attacks problems.

这个员工主动地解决问题。

2. Whenever something goes wrong, this employee searches for a solution immediately.

每当出现问题，这个员工会立刻寻找解决方法。

3. Whenever there is a chance to get actively involved, this employee

takes it.

每当有机会积极参与时,这个员工会抓住机会。

4. This employee takes initiative immediately even when others don't.

这个员工会立即采取主动,即使别人不这样做的时候。

5. This employee uses opportunities quickly in order to attain my goals.

为了实现目标,这个员工会快速把握机会。

6. Usually this employee does more than he or she is asked to do.

通常这个员工会做的比要求的多。

7. This employee is particularly good at realizing ideas

这个员工特别擅长实现构想。

Abusive supervision

1. My immediate supervisor ridicules me. *

我的直接主管会嘲笑我。

2. My immediate supervisor tells me my thoughts or feelings are stupid. *

我的直接主管会说我的想法愚蠢。

3. My immediate supervisor gives me the silent treatment.

我的直接主管对我沉默不语。

4. My immediate supervisor puts me down in front of others. *

我的直接主管会在其他人面前贬低我。

5. My immediate supervisor invades my privacy.

我的直接主管侵犯我的个人隐私。

6. My immediate supervisor reminds me of my past mistakes and failures.

我的直接主管会提醒我过去犯的错误和失败。

7. My immediate supervisor doesn't give me credit for jobs requiring a lot of effort.

即使我付出大量的努力,我的直接主管也不会称赞我的工作。

8. My immediate supervisor blames me to save himself/herself embarrassment.

APPENDIX B

我的直接主管会责备我以转移他或她自己在工作中的尴尬。

9. My immediate supervisor breaks promises he/she makes.

我的直接主管不信守承诺。

10. My immediate supervisor expresses anger at me when he/she is mad for another reason.

我的直接主管在为别的事情气恼时，会迁怒于我。

11. My immediate supervisor makes negative comments about me to others. *

我的直接主管向别人发表关于我的负面评论。

12. My immediate supervisoris rude to me.

我的直接主管对我态度粗鲁。

13. My immediate supervisor does not allow me to interact with my coworkers.

我的直接主管不允许我与同事交流。

14. My immediate supervisor tells me I'm incompetent. *

我的直接主管说我工作能力不行。

15. My immediate supervisor lies to me.

我的直接主管对我撒谎。

(Notes: Items with an asterisk were used in Study 1)

Organizational identification

1. When someone criticizes (name of company), it feels like a personal insult.

当某人批评公司时，我感觉那也是对我个人的一种攻击。

2. I am very interested in what others think about (name of company).

我对其他人怎么看待公司十分感兴趣。

3. When I talk about this company, I usually say "we" rather than "they".

当我与别人谈及公司时，我经常用"我们"而不是"他们"。

4. This company's successes are my successes.

公司的成功就是我的成功。

5. When someone praises this company, it feels like a personal compliment.
当某人赞扬公司时,我感觉那也是对我个人的称赞。

6. If a story in the media criticized the company, I would feel embarrassed.
当媒体的报道批评公司时,我会感到局促不安。

Positive affectivity

1. active
积极的

2. determined
有决心的

3. attentive
专心的

4. inspired
有创见的

5. alert
警觉的

APPENDIX C

Regression Results for Control Variables and Personal Initiative in Study 1

Model	Personal initiative		
	b	s. e.	t
Model 1			
Age	0.01	0.01	1.20
Gender	-0.09	0.11	-0.83
Education	0.12	0.06	1.92
Tenure with organization	-0.01	0.01	-0.64
Tenure with supervisor	0.07	0.07	1.08
Model 2			
Age	0.02	0.01	1.91
Gender	-0.10	0.11	-0.94
Education	0.15*	0.06	2.48
Tenure with organization	-0.02	0.01	-1.74
Tenure with supervisor	0.10*	0.05	2.03
Model 3			
Age	0.02	0.01	1.96
Gender	-0.08	0.11	-0.77
Education	0.13*	0.06	2.22
Tenure with organization	-0.02	0.01	-1.89
Tenure with supervisor	0.10*	0.05	2.11

Notes: N = 165.

* $p < 0.05$.

Regression Results for Control Variables and Proactive Behavior in Study 2

Step	OPB	SPB	CPB
Step 1			
Age	−0.01	0.03	0.06
Gender	−0.01	0.04	0.04
Education	0.07	−0.00	0.03
Tenure with organization	−0.04	−0.03	−0.13
Tenure with supervisor	0.03	0.04	0.02
Step 2			
Age	−0.00	0.03	0.07
Gender	−0.00	0.05	0.04
Education	0.08	0.01	0.03
Tenure with organization	−0.05	−0.04	−0.14
Tenure with supervisor	0.04	0.04	0.02
Step 3			
Age	−0.01	0.02	0.06
Gender	0.02	0.07	0.06
Education	0.08	0.02	0.04
Tenure with organization	−0.05	−0.04	−0.14
Tenure with supervisor	0.04	0.04	0.03

Notes: N = 226.

POSTSCRIPT

The present book is finally finished. I feel relieved at this very moment. Since joining the doctoral program of City University of Hong Kong, I went through a typical tough process of finding research topics, learning how to analyze data and writing a manuscript. Fortunately, I timely seized the opportunity for the fast development of abusive supervision research. And then things like reviewing the literature, conducting field surveys, and organizing findings etc. were quite interesting and smooth. With the completion of the study, I got my doctor's degree. This book perfectly summarizes what I have learned within the five years and shows the beginning of my further studies.

This study is financially supported by the youth program of National Natural Science Foundation of China, titled "How will a supervisor react to subordinate proactive behavior? Integrating theory on social impact and goal congruence" (71802046). and the Fundamental Research Funds for the Central Universities, titled "A dual-path model linking self-construal to well-being among university students" (2242020S20068). This book expresses my heartfelt appreciation to them. This study has received lots of help. Firstly, I would like to give my sincerest and greatest thanks to my supervisors, Dr. Shuming Zhao and Dr. Andrew Chan. They have provided patient guidance and encouragement during the completion of this study. I am also very grateful to Dr. Jenny Lee and Dr. Dong Li, etc. for their invaluable support and deep inspirations throughout my time at City

University and now at Southeast University. With their assistance and friendship, I can both concentrate on the research and enjoy my life during this study. Furthermore, I would like to thank all of the participants in the study for their support and valuable suggestions. My most special thanks are reserved for my family for their unconditional support, trust and love.

When this book is published, I would also like to thank the Economic Management Publishing House, especially Ms. Yarong Zhao. This book sincerely thanks her for her help and support in the editing process.

Finally, in the writing process of this book, a large number of domestic and foreign research results have been referred to. I would like to express my sincere thanks to the authors of these studies.

With limited research capability and time, the study in this book has several unneglectable shortcomings and limitations as well. Comments, criticisms and corrections are all welcome.